Cooking with FIVE SENSES

Cooking with FIVE SENSES

by Rita Bumbaca

Published by:
Rockmead Investments Ltd., 1990

First Published: *December 1990*

Published By: **Rockmead Investments Ltd., 1990**
               Cookbook Division
               2912 Bloor Street West
               Toronto, Ontario
               M8X 1B6

ISBN 0-9694960-0-1

Author & Registered Owner: Rita Bumbaca

The Author wishes to acknowledge the following in the development of this project:

Editor: *Rebecca Chua*
Photographer: *Paul Yelle*
Home Economist: *Arlene M. Gryfe, M.A.*

Designed & Produced by The M2000 Group
Special Design Contribution by Franca Lucci of Maleda Limited

Printed in Canada

TABLE OF CONTENTS

Menu Section

ACKNOWLEDGEMENT

*I would like to acknowledge the encouragement, support and help of the many people
without whom this book would not have been completed:*

Francesco and Maria Gallo, my father and mother

Federico Bumbaca, my husband

Concetta Bumbaca, my mother-in-law

Joseph & Michele Bumbaca, my husband's brothers

*Riccardo, Domenico and Leonardo Bumbaca,
my three sons who were often my sternest critics*

*Cecilia, my sister, and her husband Giuseppe Pellegrino,
their daughter Tania, and their two sons*

Rosa Gallo, my sister-in-law, and her daughter, Maria Luciana

*Giulia Gallo, my niece, Leo Gallo, my brother,
his wife Maria and their family,*

*and all my friends and clients
who have been asking me to write
my own cookbook for years.*

THIS BOOK IS DEDICATED
TO MY MOTHER

MARIA GALLO

Cooking with FIVE SENSES

By Rita Bumbaca

Cooking is not just whipping up a delicious meal. It's using each of five precious senses:

Sight:

    To select nature's goodness

Touch:

    To feel the texture of food

Taste:

    To distinguish among sweet, sour, bitter or tart, so you can decide whether to add a little more or a little less

Smell:

    To savour the many aromas of different meats, seafood, vegetables or pasta as they are being cooked

Hearing:

    To hear the hiss of steam or sizzle of oil in a pan as food is being cooked

Rita Bumbaca's Story

Her Kitchen suggests a cornucopia of aromas, the kind that come from memories of delicious meals and expectations of others to come; the anticipation of mouth-watering desserts, and the ever-present scent of a welcoming brew. Her kitchen is one her mother (who taught her many of her own secret recipes) would be proud of. There are breads and pastas in different corners, and cheeses in the refrigerator. Rita makes her own prosciutto, preserves, pickles and jams. But taking pride of place in her cupboard are jars of herbs, all lovingly grown and painstakingly dried, by Rita herself.

Every Italian girl is brought up to be a good cook. But Rita went far beyond just being content with the rave reviews of enthusiastic dinner guests. For her, it was important not merely to cook well, but to delve into the intricacies of Italian cuisine. Perhaps it was an innate and lively sense of curiosity which had possessed her since childhood, or perhaps it was the abundance of natural herbs that grew at the monastery on the boundaries of their properties, where the herbs were used for different remedies.

In the old days, you were supposed to accept every herbal remedy unquestioningly. "Take it, it's good for you," they would say. Well, that wasn't enough for Rita. Personal research was to prove that these herbs were good not only for flavouring and decorating, but that they also had curative powers. Today, Rita cultivates her own herbal garden and uses more than 175 herbs in cooking.

There's a popular misconception that Italian food is too rich but Rita is extremely conscious of the health aspects of cooking, and makes judicious use of herbs to achieve an important balance between health and flavour. She discovered that these same herbs provided that distinctive flavour to the regional cuisine. And, over the years, she has tried to faithfully reproduce many of the recipes that have been handed down through the generations, from her grandmother to her mother, and now to her.

Meal times were special in their household, and in compiling the recipes for this cookbook, Rita is trying to recreate a time for the family to gather and to savour the special tastes and aromas associated with the traditional foods of her childhood. But when it comes to cooking, she's adventurous, adding a little something, or subtracting, or even multiplying - just to get that elusive chemistry in her combination of ingredients to make each dish a sure winner!

Well, it's easy for Rita, you say. Some people have it, and others don't. And Rita was probably born with a flair for it. Yet those who have been seduced by her fine cuisine will probably laugh in disbelief when she confesses, "The first time I cooked, I nearly burned the kitchen".

It's true. "I was trying to make this summer dish of peas and home-made macaroni that is popular in Italy," she recalls. "I was only 16, it was my first summer in Toronto, and I was all alone at home. I was going to surprise my father and sister for dinner. I had just sautéd some onions in hot oil, and must have been adding some wet peas when - pouf! there was a gust of flame! It's a good thing I wasn't on fire too!" she laughs disarmingly.

A lesser mortal might have vowed never to set foot in the kitchen ever again. But Rita not only went right on cooking, she went on to earn kudos for her culinary skills. So popular is her cooking that many have clamoured for classes. Naturally, she obliges, having them weekly, some classes in the spring, others in the summer.

You might think that someone who can cook as well as Rita is practically a slave to her kitchen. But, having been a career woman and a successful hairdresser in her own right, Rita says, ''I don't believe in spending hours and hours in the kitchen. All I need is just 25 minutes to cook. If I'm going to spend longer than half an hour in the kitchen, I'll cook two meals, one for now and the other I will freeze for later.''

''And another thing, I'm a very practical cook - and economical too,'' she adds. Whether she's preparing a lavish spread to entertain business contacts or just a simple meal for the family, she believes in working to a budget. This poses a tremendous challenge to her creative instincts, but invariably she rises to the occasion. After all, if the cost of cooking is going to be exorbitant, you might as well dine out. But Rita is convinced that the key to a good and enjoyable meal is entertaining at home. With a modest expenditure, the inventive chef can achieve a friendly and intimate setting that would rival the most expensive restaurant; yet allow people to get to know each other better in the cosy intimacy of the home.

Perhaps the most eloquent testimony to her prowess came at one of the informal gatherings she once had. Her husband Federico, a prominent Toronto hairstylist, sailed into this meeting and, quite unprompted, announced to the class, ''You know, I will never leave my wife because of her superb cooking!''

Rita points out that the husband-and-wife team complement each other not only in the hairdressing salon but also in the kitchen. Federico's specialty is barbecued meat and fish. He imbues the sauces with a distinctive zing and is a great one for salad - after all, he does a mean coleslaw!

As for Rita, she has every recipe for a happy household, particularly with three strapping, appreciative sons. She has so many recipes that her calendar of cuisine is truly one for all seasons. As a bonus, she even provides some menus for entertaining.

Rebecca Chua
Editor

Herbs Used in Cooking with Five Senses

Angelica
Used in Syrups, Teas

Basil
Used in Eggplants, Tomatoes, Potatoes

Bay Leaves
Used in Figs, Soups, Teas,
Preserving

Borage
Used in Soups, Stuffings, Teas

Caraway
Used in Stuffing, Breads, Fish, Pork

Chervil
Used in Delicate Fishes, Lobster

Chives
Used in Cold Salads, Frittata, Baking

Coriander
Used in Meats, Pickling

Comfrey
Used in Stuffings, Soups,
Vegetables, Teas

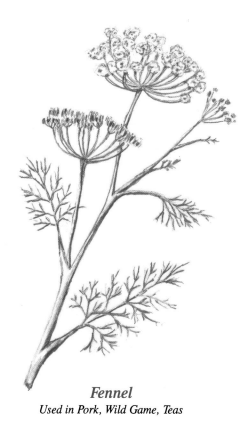

Fennel
Used in Pork, Wild Game, Teas

Hyssop
Used in Dressings, Vinegars, Marinade
for Pork, Veal, Chicken

Juniper
Used in Soups, Sauces, Pork, Beef

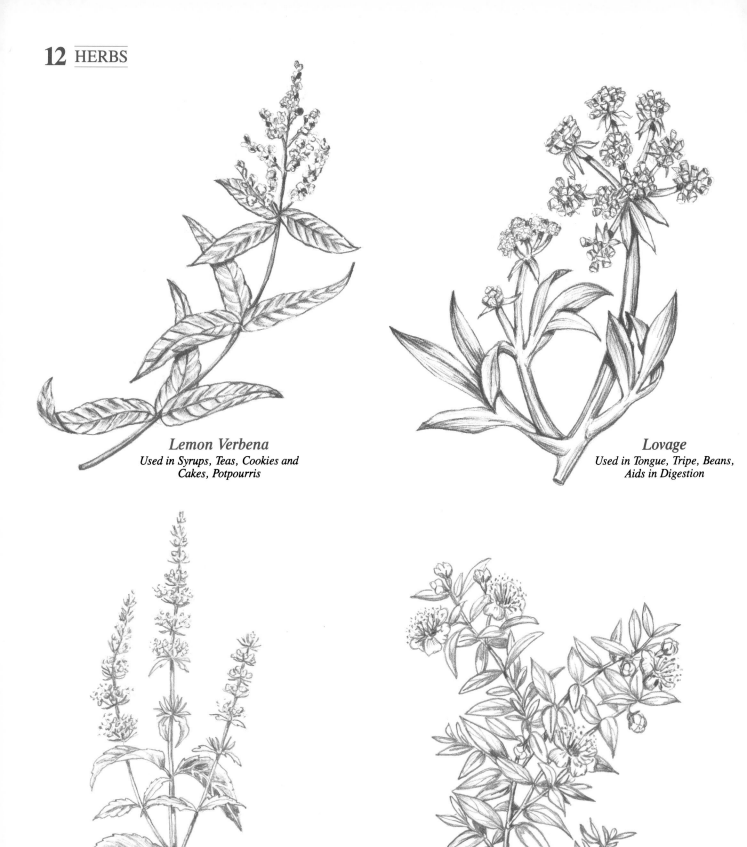

Lemon Verbena
Used in Syrups, Teas, Cookies and Cakes, Potpourris

Lovage
Used in Tongue, Tripe, Beans, Aids in Digestion

Mint
Used in Teas, Sauces and Peas

Myrtle
Used in Soups, Cabbage, Pork, Beef, Game, Tea

Oregano
*Used in Tomatoes, Eggplant,
Mushrooms*

Parsley
*Used in Fish, Chicken, Soups and
Pasta*

Pineapple Sage
Used in Syrups, Teas, Potpourris

Rosemary
*Used in Teas, Baked Potatoes, Pork,
Beef, Soothes Nerves*

Sage
Used in Chicken, Turkey, Wild Game

Savory
Used in Chicken, Turkey, Wild Game

Thyme
Used in Chicken, Eggplant, Vinegars

Tarragon
Used in Vinegars, Chicken, Eggplant

PRESERVES

Grape Syrup
Old-Fashioned Peach Jam with Angelica
Yellow Plum Jam
Peaches in Syrup
Canadian Pickles
Cherries in Grappa
Pickled Eggplant
Preserved Olives
Preserved Artichokes
Holy Oil
Carolina's Preserved Asparagus
Mushroom Preserve
Piquant Peppers Stuffed with Herbs
Roasted Peppers
Herbal Vinegar
Raspberry Vinegar

Grape Syrup
(Vino cotto di Rosa Gallo)

My grandmother used to take great pride in the making of vino cotto as that was what distinguished a traditional Italian household. Each family had its own grape syrup, one made from white wine and the other from red wine, and the making of these was a closely-guarded secret.

Vino cotto is used to sweeten much of the Traditional Christmas fare. In the winter, snow was sweetened with vino cotto as a dessert. It is also used as a topping for bread and to sweeten drinks.

Method

In the summer when the grapes were harvested, the sweetest grapes, ones that were savoured for their bouquet, were picked. My grandmother would save the first juice squeezed from those grapes, and sieve them through a fine muslin cloth.

She would pour the juice into a pan and use a wooden spoon to mark the thirds. This juice was then boiled until it was reduced by a third.

She stored the resulting vino cotto in clean bottles. They will keep well from year to year. ❖

Old-fashioned Peach Jam with Angelica
(Marmellata di pesche all'angelica)

Ingredients

6	32-oz jars
23	peaches
5	cups sugar
6	lemons, juice only
1	branch angelica
2	cooking apples, peeled
1	branch lemon sage

Method

Place peaches in boiling water for 2-3 minutes. Remove from heat. Peel skin off and cut into pieces. Squeeze the juice of 1 lemon on peaches and sprinkle 5 cups of sugar on top. Do not stir. Let stand for 1 hour.

After an hour, stir peaches and pour the peach juice into a pot. To get good results, use a low wide stainless steel pot. Cook for 5 minutes on medium heat, stirring with a wooden spoon. Add peaches, whole apples, branch of angelica, lemon sage and the rest of the lemon juice stirring over medium heat. A foam will form. Keep stirring until foam disappears and it becomes glossy. This is an old-fashioned indication that the jam is ready.

Remove the angelica and apple cores. Sterilize jars by placing them in the oven at 150° for 20 minutes. Pour boiling jam into jars. Put new lids on jars and store in a cool, dark place. ❖

Yellow Plum Jam
(Marmellata di susine)

To make good jam, you need about 3/4 ripe plums and a 1/4 of firm ones. But if you happen to have bought all ripe plums, just add a peeled cooking apple to the plums as they cook.

Ingredients

5	12-oz jars
12	cups tiny yellow plums
6	cups sugar
	rind of 1 lemon
	juice of 3 lemons,

Method

Wash and remove the pits of the plums. Place in a dish. Add juice of 2 lemons.

In a wide stainless steel frying pan, cook the plums and lemon juice over medium heat. Add rind. A foam will form. Add juice of other lemon about 5 minutes later. Keep stirring for 10-15 minutes until foam disappears and it becomes glossy. This is an old-fashioned indication that the jam is ready.

Remove the apple core. Sterilize jars by placing them in the oven at 150° F for 20 minutes. Pour boiling jam into jars. Put new lids on jars and store in a cool, dark place. ❖

Peaches in Syrup

(Pesche sciroppate)

This recipe involves the entire family. We make a special trip to Niagara Falls and buy about three bushels of firm peaches. Each one of our family is kept busy: one washes, one peels, another slices and I do the packing.

For this recipe, you need to keep an eye on the syrup, because the liquid evaporates as it boils. My family does not like the peaches too sweet, but you may vary the amount of sugar to suit your own tastes. Also be sure that there are no draughts when you start working.

Preserving Ingredients

16	32-oz sterilized jars
9	quarts water
2	cups sugar
1	branch angelica
4	bay leaves
8	rose-lemon geranium leaves
1	bushel Gold Jubilee peaches, washed, peeled and quartered
7	pints water
	juice of 3 lemons
2	Tbsp sugar

Method

Place jars in oven at 150° F. Take them out one at a time.

Boil first 5 ingredients (not including jars) to make packing syrup. Keep covered at boiling point.

In another pan, bring water, lemon juice and sugar to a boil. When the water is boiling, add 5 cups of peaches. When it starts to bubble again, remove with a slotted spoon.

Remove jar from oven and fill with peaches. Shake the jar so that peaches will settle. Place wooden spoon sideways inside the mouth of jar and drain excess water back into pan.

Take a cup of the packing syrup and fill jar up to 1" from the brim. Wipe surface of jar with clean cloth. Seal tightly with new lid. Cover with towel.

Store covered with an old sheet or in a box. This keeps in a dark place for up to 2 years.

Hint: I usually save the peach pits and skins to make peach juice by boiling them with the remaining syrup. Bring to boil. Sieve through strainer and place in sterilized jars. ❖

Canadian Pickles

(Cetriolini alla canadese)

Ingredients

10	32-oz jars
10	garlic cloves
10	branches dill
12	cups water
12	cups white vinegar
2	branches tarragon
2	branches thyme
4	bay leaves
4	branches savory
5	Tbsp salt
1	basket small cucumbers

Method

Wash and cover the small cucumbers with cold water. Empty 3 trays of ice into the water and keep cool for 3 hours. Drain in a colander.

Place one garlic clove and dill in each jar. Place remaining ingredients in a large, heavy saucepan and boil for 2-3 minutes.

Place 6-7 cucumbers in each jar, filling them with the boiled liquid. Seal tightly and store in a cool, dark place so pickles will not discolour. Let stand for a month to allow flavours to blend before opening. ❖

Cherries in Grappa

(Ciliege alla grappa)

Ingredients

2	lbs firm black cherries
	Grappa, Brandy or Cognac

Method

Remove stems and rinse cherries. Dry well and place in a jar. Top with Grappa, Brandy or Cognac. Cover tightly.

 ❖

Pickled Eggplant
(Melanzane all'aceto)

Women's liberation came very early to the South of Italy, as the men were involved in the pickling of eggplant, making breads and preparing sausages and hams, even in making tomato sauce, longer than I can remember.

This recipe draws upon a man's brute strength because he would squeeze the water out of the eggplants until they were absolutely dry. But there is another way of doing it.

Ingredients

11	large eggplants
1	cup coarse salt
2	stalks celery, cut into thin 2" lengths
4	sweet pepper, julienne
4	hot peppers, cut into rounds
4	oz red vinegar
1	Tbsp salt

Method

Wash and peel eggplants, and cut them into 1" lengths. After cutting, sprinkle salt over and place in a large dish.

Cover with a dish and put a stack of dishes weighing about 10 lbs over it. Turn eggplants after about 2 hours and replace weight on top. Leave for 12 hours.

Drain eggplants in a colander. Place weight on top for 1-1/2 hours. Turn every so often and replace weight until eggplants are completely dry.

Remove eggplant to smaller dish. Cover with white vinegar. Replace weight on top. Let stand for 24 hours.

Drain eggplants in a colander. Place weight on top for 1-1/2 hours. Turn eggplants after 2 hours until they are completely dry.

Put remaining 5 ingredients in a dish. Stir and leave for 5 minutes. Drain.

Dressing

6	garlic cloves, quartered
20	mint leaves
1	Tbsp thyme
1	cup sweet basil
1	Tbsp peppercorn
3	Tbsp red vinegar
2	oz olive oil

1	Tbsp olive oil and vinegar for the top of each jar

Mix the eggplant and dressing well. Pack very tightly into 6 jars with a wooden spoon. Add mixture of 1 Tbsp oil and vinegar to the top of each. Add more oil if necessary before sealing well. Keep in a cool dark place. ❖

Preserved Olives
(Olive in salamoia)

These are plain olives which can be eaten as is, or added to salads and other dishes to dress them up.

Ingredients

4	32-oz jars
1	case large yellowish to purplish Spanish olives
1	cup coarse salt
5	quarts water

Method

Make 6 cuts lengthwise from the top to the bottom in each of the olives. Place in a pan of cold water. Change water twice a day.

After 4 days, drain water. Add cup of salt. Let stand for 3-4 hours, turning every now and then with a wooden spoon.

Drain olives in a colander. Bring 12 cups of water to boil. Cool completely.

Fill jars with olives. Add water so that the tops are completely covered. Seal with new lids. Store in a cool, dark place. These will keep for a year or so. ❖

Preserved Artichokes

(Carciofi all'aceto)

Artichokes grew in great abundance in Rogliano, where I grew up. They were fried, stuffed and steamed, and served with chicken, veal or salad. The little artichokes were often served with spaghetti sauce. They were also fried with onions and eggs to make frittata.

The dark leaves of the artichoke were also washed and dried to make tea. About 15 leaves were usually put in a tea pot, and boiling water poured over it. This was recommended for those anaemic in health.

This recipe was passed down the generations from my great-grandmother. In Canada, the best artichokes are available at the end of April or early in May.

Ingredients

1	case fresh Californian artichokes (approx. 65)
2	32-oz or 4 16-oz jars

Cleaning the Artichokes

Remove all the dark green leaves. Peel the stem of the artichoke which is its heart. Trim at an angle, keeping the pyramid shape of the artichoke. Quarter or halve them according to size. Place them in cold water with half a lemon. The best way to keep artichokes from darkening is to clean each artichoke carefully step by step before proceeding to the next.

Brine

12	cups water
12	cups white vinegar
1	tsp mustard seed
1	tsp coriander
1	tsp black peppercorns
4	red peppercorns
1	tsp juniper berries
4	garlic cloves, quartered
1	tsp rosemary
1	Tbsp salt

Method

In a large pot, bring all the brine ingredients to a boil. Simmer for 2-3 minutes. Add the artichokes and cook for 3 minutes or until they turn a greeny yellow. Drain in a colander. Put a weight on them and let sit until cool.

Dressing

2	cups mint leaves
1	cup parsley
10	garlic cloves
2	hot green peppers
5	branches tarragon, leaves only
3	branches hyssop, leaves only
5	branches savory, leaves only
5	branches thyme, leaves only
1	oz olive oil

Method

In a large dish, place the artichokes and all other dressing ingredients. Toss and pack in jars with a wooden spoon, making sure there is no air in the jars.

Let stand for 2 hours without lids and add more oil if necessary. Cover with new lids. Keeps up to a year in a cool place. ❖

Holy Oil

(Olio santo)

This is my family's very old recipe which helps digestion, and is used for flavouring salad, steamed vegetables and legumes.

Ingredients

32	oz extra virgin olive oil
2	fresh bay leaves, washed and dried
2	dried hot peppers
1	branch fresh rosemary
10	juniper berries
1	tsp raspberry vinegar

Place all ingredients in a bottle. Shake well. Leave on a sunny window sill for a week or two.

Store in a dark place. After a month, it will have an even better flavour. Remove herbs, when ready to use. ❖

Carolina's Preserved Asparagus

(Asparaci alla Carolina)

Preserving asparagus usually turns out to be a family enterprise because we buy a whole case of asparagus and we share the fruits of our labour. They are excellent for a buffet or as a barbecue accompaniment.

Ingredients

8	32-oz sterilized jars
30	lbs asparagus
5	quarts water
10	cups white vinegar
2	garlic cloves
2	Tbsp savory
2	bay leaves
2	Tbsp red pepper
1/2	cup salt

Method

Place asparagus in cold water with salt. Let stand for 1/2 hour. Rinse.

Bring the last 7 ingredients to boil in a large spaghetti pan. Tie 1/3 asparagus and cook with tips up in brine for 3 minutes until their colour changes, as they should be crunchy to the taste. Remove and place in a colander.

Continue with remaining 2/3 until all asparagus has been cooked. Cool completely. Place in a dish.

Dressing

2	cups olive oil
1	cup tarragon vinegar
8	garlic cloves, quartered
1	cup parsley leaves
2	Tbsp black peppercorns

Combine 1/2 of olive oil and vinegar, all the garlic, parsley and peppercorns to the asparagus. Toss like a salad.

Pack jars tightly with asparagus. Add rest of the oil and vinegar to the top of each jar. Make sure there is enough oil on the surface. Seal tight.

Store in a cool, dark place.

Mushroom Preserve

(Funghi alla silana)

This is a very useful preserve which can be used as an antipasto or served with artichoke, meat or fish. It can keep for up to a year if the recipe is faithfully followed.

Brine Ingredients

1	16-oz jar
2	lbs mushrooms, cleaned and washed
1	celery stalk cut into thin 2" lengths
2	sweet peppers, julienned
2	hot peppers, cut into rounds
1	quart water
2-1/4	cups white vinegar
3	garlic cloves
1	Tbsp salt
1	sprig tarragon
1/2	tsp hot pepper
1/2	tsp oregano

Method

Place last 7 ingredients in a pot and boil for 1 minute. Add mushrooms, celery, sweet and hot peppers, stirring for 2 minutes until they change colour.

Drain in a colander. Place a stack of dishes on top to weigh it down. After 1/2 hour, stir with your hand. Replace dishes on top. In the meantime mix the dressing as follows.

Dressing

2	garlic cloves, quartered
20	mint leaves
1	Tbsp thyme
2	oz olive oil
1	Tbsp olive oil or vinegar for the top of the jar

Put all ingredients in a dish, add vegetables. Mix well. Pack very tightly into the jar with a wooden spoon. Add 1 Tbsp oil or vinegar to the top. Add more oil if necessary before sealing well. Keep in a cool, dark place. ❖

Piquant Peppers Stuffed with Herbs

(Peperoncini piccanti ripieni all'erbe)

Brine Ingredients

16	red and green hot and round peppers
12	medium mushrooms, cleaned
4	cups water
2	cups white vinegar
1	garlic clove
1	branch tarragon
1	branch savory
6	coriander seeds
3	leaves sage
2	branches thyme
2	Tbsp salt

Before using, leave hot peppers overnight at room temperature. You should use gloves when cleaning them. Cut round the top and remove core and seeds.

Boil last 9 ingredients for 5 minutes.

Place mushrooms in brine for 1-2 minutes. Remove with a slotted spoon. Drain well and chop.

Place peppers in brine for 1-2 minutes. Remove with a slotted spoon and place upside down on paper towels to cool.

Stuffing

1	14-oz can pitted green olives, chopped
4	fillets anchovies
4	Tbsp capers, rinsed and chopped
8	almonds, grated
3	pecans, grated
1/2	cup parsley, chopped
1	tsp fresh thyme
2	tsp fresh savory
1	Tbsp tarragon
2	Tbsp fresh basil, chopped

Method

Place all ingredients in a bowl, add mushrooms and mix well. Stuff peppers with mixture. Place in jars and cover with oil. This will keep for up to 3 months refrigerated. Before serving, drain on paper towels. ❖

Roasted Peppers

(Peperoni Arrostiti sul B.B.Q.)

Most Italian families make bushels of these roasted peppers because they are a delicious appetizer. They are very versatile, in antipasto, as a side-dish, or in sandwiches, and even as a barbecue accompaniment. They are also rich in vitamins B and C.

Ingredients

4	big green peppers
2	hot peppers
2	yellow or red peppers

Method

Wash and dry peppers. When the barbecue is hot, place peppers stem side down on top of grill and cook. Keep turning peppers until skins bubble. Remove, let cool and either serve or store in freezer bags.

To serve, peel, remove seeds and slice lengthwise, and mix with either of the following dressings.

Mild Dressing

2	garlic cloves, quartered
10	sprigs parsley
1/4	tsp sugar
4-5	sweet basil leaves, minced
4-5	mint leaves, minced
1/2	tsp oregano
1	oz olive oil

Piquant Dressing

2	tsp fresh thyme
10	fresh tarragon leaves
1	Tbsp fresh savory
1	Tbsp fresh hyssop
1	oz olive oil

For either dressing, mix all ingredients together and pour over peppers. ❖

Herbal Vinegar
(Aceto all'erbe)

Herbal vinegar tastes much better when it is aged for at least two years. I have faithfully reproduced my grandmother's recipe. The beauty of this vinegar is that it aids in the digestion.

Ingredients

4	32-oz bottles
5	quarts white wine vinegar
2	branches tarragon
1	branch hyssop
2	branches savory
1	branch sage
2	branches thyme
2	bay leaves

Method

Rinse all herbs in cold water and dry well. Place in vinegar. Shake well. Seal tightly. Place in a sunny spot outside during the summer for 1 month. Remember to shake it once a day.

Filter it and replace with same combination of herbs. Replace in sunny spot for another month, shaking it once a day.

Repeat for third month.

Store in a dark place for the winter months.

In the summer, repeat the process.

In the fall, filter and bottle. In each bottle, add 1 branch of the herb of your choice. Seal tightly and store. ❖

Raspberry Vinegar
(Aceto di lamponi)

Ingredients

4	32-oz bottles
5	quarts white wine vinegar
1	pint raspberries, rinsed and dried
10	raspberry leaves

Method

Place raspberries and leaves in vinegar. Shake well. Seal tightly. Place in a sunny spot outside. Remember to shake it once a day.

After 10 days, filter and replace with fresh raspberries. Replace at least 3 times during the raspberry season.

Store in a dark place for the winter months.

In the summer, repeat the process.

In the fall, filter and bottle. In each bottle, add a few fresh raspberries and leaves. Seal tightly and store. ❖

Preserved Fruit with Angelica Syrup
Cherries in Grappa
Recipe page 17

TRADITIONAL RECIPES

Many of the recipes found here have been handed down from generation to generation, and are very old. They were passed down from my grandmother to my mother, and from my mother to me.

But, as most of these recipes were transmitted orally, I have tried and tested these recipes many times for the exact measurements needed in the cookbook.

I have made minimal changes, such as substituting butter for lard, which was often used in baking and frying, and is much heavier. Fortunately, practically all the ingredients I use are available here in Canada. These recipes are much healthier but they taste exactly the same as the favourite meals of my childhood.

Papa's Meatballs

(Polpette di Papà)

Serves 12

This was the first recipe my father ever taught me. When I was only three or four years old, he made me memorize all the ingredients, so I could help my mother make them. These meatballs freeze very well.

You can take a little piece the shape of a hazelnut, shape them into little balls and stuff them with rice. Or you can make flat oval pieces about 3" long and 2" wide, and they can be served fried. Alternatively, you can make meatballs the size of half an orange, and add to soup. They only take about 20 minutes to cook and are simply delicious!

Ingredients

1	lb pork
1	lb veal
5	eggs
1	cup breadcrumbs
2	cups goat or parmiggiano cheese
1	Tbsp parsley, chopped
1	garlic clove, minced
2	Tbsp fresh basil, chopped
1/4	tsp black pepper
1/4	tsp cayenne
1	tsp salt
1/4	cup red or white wine
1/2	cup olive oil

Method

Mix all the ingredients except oil in a bowl and knead with your hands. Let rest at room temperature for at least half an hour.

Make sure you use a non-stick frying pan. Shape the meatballs into preferred sizes. Place them into sizzling olive oil. Shake the pan a little, and, just before they turn brown, take them out with a slotted spoon. Place in tomato sauce and serve with home-made pasta.

If you prefer not to fry them first, you may roll them and place them straight away into simmering sauce or soup. ❖

Old-Fashioned Meat Sauce

(Ragù)

Serves 8

Ingredients

2	lbs goat, chopped
1	lb pork shoulder, chopped
1/4	cup oil
2	bay leaves
1	branch rosemary
1	onion, chopped
4	garlic cloves
1/4	cup red wine
1	hot pepper
4	Tbsp parsley, chopped
2	cans tomatoes, sieved
1	can tomato paste
	salt to taste

Method

In a pot, place all ingredients except the parsley, tomatoes and tomato paste. Cook for 5 minutes covered, over low heat, stirring occasionally.

Uncover and cook until meat is golden. Add tomato paste and continue stirring. Add tomatoes and salt to taste. Simmer for 20-30 minutes.

Just before serving, add parsley. ❖

Old-Fashioned Ravioli

Serves 14

My mother used to make her ravioli by hand, which accounted for the difference in the sizes of each which she served only on special occasions. Nowadays, pasta machines yield much more uniform sizes, but this does not change the taste.

This recipe makes 150 ravioli for a party of 30. Freeze the remainder.

Ingredients for the Dough

12	eggs
7	cups all-purpose flour
1/2	cup milk
1	cup flour for rolling

Method

Place flour on pasta board. Make a well in the centre and add slightly beaten eggs. Blend eggs into flour with a rotating motion. Add milk only if mixture is too dry.

Knead dough for 10 minutes or until soft and smooth. Place in a dish and cover with a linen cloth. Let stand at room temperature for 10 minutes, as you prepare the filling.

Ingredients for Filling

2	lbs lean pork, ground twice
2	lbs lean veal, ground twice
1/2	cup white wine
3	Tbsp breadcrumbs
1	cup grated parmiggiano Reggiano cheese
1/4	tsp allspice
1/2	tsp fresh ground black pepper
2	Tbsp fresh basil
4	fresh minced green onions, white parts only
4	garlic cloves, minced
2	eggs for later use
	salt to taste
	oil to cover the bottom of pan

Method

Barely cover the bottom of a pan with oil. Sauté onions, garlic and meat on low heat. Do not brown. Gently mix in white wine, breadcrumbs, basil, salt, pepper and allspice, turning for about one minute, making sure that the filling does not dry up. Remove from heat and let cool. Mix in two raw eggs and cheese.

Take a piece of dough the size of an egg and flatten with the palms of your hands. Put through pasta machine at #1, then again at #2 and so on to #5. Each strip should be 20" long. Lay on the table and place filling 1 tsp for every 2".

Fold over and seal with your hands, then cut with the ravioli cutter.

Bring a large pot of cold water to boil, adding salt to taste. Cook ravioli for 10 minutes. Drain.

Serve ravioli with pesto sauce, red sauce or with butter and parmiggiano cheese. As an appetizer, serve 5-6 per person. For the main course, serve 10-12 per person.

To store the remaining ravioli, freeze for later use. Do not refrigerate as the dough has a tendency to stick to one another.

TO FREEZE, place parchment paper on tray, then place ravioli in freezer until completely frozen. Do this with each batch until all are completely frozen. Take out from the freezer and pack into freezer bags. To prevent freezer burn, double the bags and date them. Ensure that they are air-tight and they will keep for 3-4 months.
For quick preparation, remove ravioli frozen from the freezer and add to boiling water, with 2 Tbsp of olive oil and salt to taste. ❖

Old-fashioned Tomato Sauce

(Salsa di pomodoro)

Serves 12

Ingredients

4	28-oz cans plum tomatoes, sieved
1	5-1/2-oz can tomato paste
1	onion, chopped very fine
2	garlic cloves, chopped very fine
1/2	cup olive oil
2	bay leaves
1	small hot pepper (optional)
2	Tbsp fresh basil

Put oil in pan with bay leaves, onions and garlic and lightly stir for a few minutes. Add tomato paste and plum tomatoes. Bring to boil. Gently add the meatballs and simmer for 20-25 minutes. Just before serving, add basil. ❖

Braciole alla Montanara

Serves 6

My grandmother used to make this dish from a preserved pork butt which she sliced into 1/2" thicknesses. After she placed the long slices in a crock pot, she would sprinkle sea salt on each one.

She would then cover the crock with a piece of wood and place a heavy rock, weighing perhaps 10 lbs. on it. The meat would keep indefinitely.

Whenever she wanted some pork, she would rinse it off with some wine and make her Braciole. This was often the "pièce de resistance" at weddings, and was served with sauce and pasta al salice, symbolizing the union of the newlyweds.

Ingredients

6	slices pork butt
6	Tbsp breadcrumbs
1	cup milk or white wine
1	white onion, white only, minced
1	garlic clove, minced
4	Tbsp parsley, minced
5	Tbsp goat or pecorino cheese
1	egg, slightly beaten
1	pig's caul 12" x 12" or tooth picks
	salt and pepper to taste

Method

Soak breadcrumbs in milk or white wine for a couple of minutes. Squeeze the liquid. Mix all ingredients together. Stuff into meat. Roll meat up, using toothpicks to hold them together, or wrap with pig's caul.

Ingredients for Tomato Sauce

3	Tbsp tomato paste
2	28-oz cans tomatoes, strained
1	small hot pepper (optional)
2	oz olive oil
1	oz wine
2	garlic cloves, chopped
1	Tbsp parsley, chopped
	salt and pepper to taste
2	lbs pasta al salice

Method

Barely cover the bottom of a sauce pan with olive oil. Add garlic. Cook braciole covered over low heat for 2-3 minutes. Uncover and let cook until golden. Add wine and shake the pan. Remove with a slotted spoon and place on platter.

In the same oil, add tomato paste and tomatoes. Simmer for 20 minutes. Add braciole, simmer for another 5 minutes. Sprinkle parsley. Remove braciole and serve as a side dish.

Serve sauce with pasta al salice. Recipe follows.

Willow Pasta

(Pasta al salice)

Serves 6-8

In the town of Montalto in the Province of Cosenza, this intricate pasta is a speciality. Its shape is acquired from being rolled round the slender branch of a willow, and this recipe was given to me by Mrs. Filomena Vannelli, my sister-in-law's mother.

Ingredients

6-1/2	cups all purpose flour
3	cups water

Method

Turn flour onto non-stick surface. Make a well in the centre. Add water, working flour with rotating motion until water is absorbed. Dough should be hard. Knead for about 10 minutes.

Roll dough into a cylindrical shape and cut into 8 pieces. Place in an air-tight container. Let rest for 1/2 hour.

Take one piece at a time. Cut into 4 sections. With your hands roll into a 1/4" diameter by 12" long. Cut again into 4" pieces. Place in tray. Repeat procedures to all other pieces. Cover.

Rub your hands with a drop of oil. Take each 4" piece, flatten and place a willow branch in the middle of the dough. Take the sides up and pinch together. Roll from inside out in a stretching motion until the texture is nice and even. Cover the branch. Remove the willow branch from the middle of the dough. Lay the rolled dough over a linen towel. Repeat until all dough is used up.

Bring to a boil in a pot 12 quarts of water, with salt to taste. Add pasta and boil for 10-12 minutes. Drain and serve with the sauce.

Herbed Tripe
(Trippa all'erbe)

Serves 6

This Italian delicacy is dedicated to my late brother Raffaele Gallo, a famous artist, who loved this dish. Today, it is very difficult to find good unbleached tripe. The last time we visited my brother in Italy, it took him three days to find the right tripe, which we cooked over an open fire.

Trippa all'erbe was the kind of dish on which Italian chefs used to stake their reputations. If you do it well, you have surpassed yourself. But it requires a lot of work and for that reason I only make this dish once a year, for my husband's close friends.

Ingredients

6	lbs tripe
3	large onions, cut into large pieces
3	lemons cut into large pieces
1	cup coarse salt

Method

Place tripe under cold running water, scouring with the help of a knife. Make sure you trim all the fat off.

Knead the onions, salt and lemon into the tripe. Rinse with cold water. Repeat three times. Let stand in cold water for about half an hour. Cut into 4"-long strips.

1	cup dry white wine
7	large potatoes, quartered
4	cups tomatoes
2	oz olive oil
1	onion, cut into pieces
4	garlic cloves
2	hot peppers
2	tsp parsley, minced
3	branches lovage
4	tsp sweet basil
4	bay leaves

Method

After rinsing, place tripe and 2 branches of lovage in a covered pan. Simmer over low heat until all the water has evaporated.

Add oil, wine, onion, bay leaves, remaining branches of lovage, salt and pepper to taste. Cook for 2-3 minutes before adding tomatoes. Turn occasionally.

Add potatoes, salt and pepper. Cook for another 1/2 hour covered until potatoes are cooked.

Sprinkle with parsley and basil. Serve with red wine and fresh cooked beans. ❖

Gnocchi with Ricotta
(Shranguglia previti)

Serves 8

This is a very old-fashioned recipe featuring potatoes, squash and cottage cheese. In my home town it was called Shranguglia Previti, which means "strangled priest" in dialect.

This recipe is dedicated to my friend Daniela Bonetta. This is her favourite request on her birthday. It is usually served with a special meat sauce, which we call Ragû.

Ingredients

1	lb fresh ricotta (2 packs) or 4 large potatoes, boiled and mashed
3	eggs
2	Tbsp butter
1	lb flour
1	cup flour (for later use)
10	pints water

Method

Place flour in the middle of a rolling board and make a well. Place the ricotta, butter and eggs in the centre. Using your hands, knead the dough until all the flour is absorbed and the dough is smooth.

Take a piece and roll it 8" long. Put aside on a floured surface. Do this to the rest of the dough until everything is finished. Cut the rolled pieces about 1" long.

Pick each piece and press lightly with the tips of your fingers against a cheese grater. Flip each piece quickly against it so that it curls and forms a little gondola landing on floured trays.

Place the gnocchi in 10 pints of boiling water. Cook for 9-12 minutes until the gnocchi float to the surface. Drain. Serve with butter and cheese or meat sauce. ❖

Meatloaf
(Polpettone della salute)

Serves 6

This very old-fashioned recipe makes 4 meatloaves. I usually serve two and freeze the other two. It can be made with any kind of meat - veal, pork or beef. You can even mix half of one kind of meat and half of another.

Ingredients

5	lbs shoulder veal, minced
1	Tbsp salt
1/4	tsp cayenne
1/4	tsp ginger
1	Tbsp winter savory
1	Tbsp basil
1	tsp sage
1/4	tsp allspice
1	cup wheatgerm
1/2	cup oats
1	cup white wine
3	green onions, white part only, chopped
4	eggs, slightly beaten
2	garlic cloves, minced
1	cup friulano cheese, grated
1	cup romano cheese
1-1/2	oz olive oil

Method

Place all ingredients in a dish large enough to hold them. Mix well with your hands. Let rest for 5 minutes. Divide into four. Shape each into an oval loaf.

Mix the following ingredients like a salad:

6	potatoes, peeled and quartered lengthwise
3	sweet potatoes, cut into three
6	slices of yellow squash
4	celery stalks, cut into 2" strips
4	medium onions, peeled and quartered
1/2	tsp rosemary
1/2	tsp paprika
	salt to taste
1	oz olive oil

Place all the above around the meatloaf in a casserole and cover. Bake 2 meatloaves for an hour at 350° F or until potatoes are cooked.

TO FREEZE: Wrap meatloaf in wax paper, then with foil. Place in freezer bag and date. Remove from freezer, unwrap wax paper and foil, and bake at 350° for 1-1/2 hours. ❖

Easter Eve Frittata
(Frittata del Santo Sabato)

Serves 6

On the Saturday following Good Friday, we used to bring bread to the church to be blessed. And whenever we got home from church, my mother would have prepared this frittata for us.

The only change I have made to this recipe is to substitute ham for the home-made prosciutto which my mother used. Sometimes, I put it in a baking dish and bake it like a quiche. But most of the time, I pan-fry and then broil it. It's excellent cold or hot for lunch.

Ingredients

4	cups zucchini, sliced finely
6	green onions, chopped
1/2	cup ham, cut small
1/2	cup fresh pecorino
1/2	cup fresh ricotta
6	eggs
2	Tbsp flour
2	Tbsp chopped parsley
1/4	cup olive oil
	salt to taste

Method

Place zucchini in a dish and sprinkle salt over. Let stand for about 10 minutes.

In a non-stick frying pan, add zucchini, ham and oil. Sauté over high heat for 1-2 minutes. Remove with a slotted spoon. Leave oil in pan.

Beat eggs, adding ricotta, pecorino, flour and parsley. Add zucchini to the egg mixture.

Place the same frying pan over medium heat. Pour mixture in, shaking for 1-2 minutes. Using the same frying pan, broil in oven until golden. ❖

Hot or Sweet Sausage

(Salciccia piccante o'dolce)

There is nothing like home-made sausage, as this old-fashioned recipe from Southern Italy demonstrates. The difference between the way that this sausage is made in my home town in Cosenza and the way it is done in Reggio is that we love sweet sausage and tend to use sweet peppers. In Reggio, however, they love fiery sausages and use hot peppers instead.

When making hot or sweet sausage, ask your friendly butcher for a little more casing than you actually need in case they burst in the process. He will also tell you how much salt you need, and provide sausage thread to tie it up.

These are great for barbecues and buffets. They can be served with polenta, made into frittata or baked with potatoes in the oven.

Ingredients for Filling

44	lbs pork shoulder and 1 butt minced by butcher
4	cups red wine
1-1/4	cup salt
1/2	cup black pepper, freshly ground (optional)
1/2	cup paprika
1-1/2	cup hot pepper or sweet pepper
3	Tbsp fennel seeds

Ingredients for Casing

1/2	cup wine
1/2	cup vinegar
	needle
	sausage thread

Preparing the Casing

In a bowl of cold water, add 1/2 cup wine and 1/2 cup vinegar. Soak casing for about half an hour. Then rinse in running cold water under faucet. Place in bowl of cold water and 1 oz vinegar. Stand for later use.

Method

Place meat on top of a clean counter and pat down 2-3" thick. Sprinkle half of the salt, pepper, wine, fennel seeds, paprika and hot or sweet pepper on top. Flip meat over and sprinkle the remaining ingredients on top. Knead well for 20 minutes until meat sticks together. Leave in a cool place overnight or for a few hours.
To see if the meat has been seasoned to your liking, pinch off a small piece and fry it. Cool and taste.

Attach a stuffing horn to the machine and push the casing into the horn and tie the end. Push the sausage mixture through the grinder with the right hand. The casing will unroll as it fills with the sausage mixture. Do not pack the sausage mixture too tightly or the casing will burst.

Prick the sausage to make sure that the air is expelled. This will prevent the sausage from darkening. Tie every 6" with thread.

Freezing

To freeze, place in heavy plastic bags wrapped with freezing paper. Tie in place with elastic band and date.

When ready to use, remove from plastic bags, thaw for 20 minutes before cooking or barbecuing. ❖

Pork Liver Sausage

(Salciccia di fegato)

Ingredients

1	lb liver cut in long thin slices
3	lbs pork butt, coarsely ground
2	garlic cloves, squeezed
5	Tbsp parsley, minced
1	Tbsp winter savory
1/2	tsp sage
1	cup red wine
	salt and pepper to taste

Preparing the Casing

(See instructions for Hot or Sweet Sausages)

Method

Place all ingredients in a bowl. Knead for 5-10 minutes. Let stand for an hour.

Casing

Proceed the same way as with the Hot or Sweet Sausage.

Sausage, Potatoes and Onions under the Ashes

(Salciccia, patate e cipolle sotto la cenere)

Serves 6

During the cold Italian winters, we would keep a fire burning in the grate for weeks, both night and day. It was then that my grandmother would prepare this simply scrumptious dish.

In those days, she used sugar paper to wrap sausages, potatoes and onions. These were actually reused sugar bags soaked in oil or lard. Over them, she would wrap five or six layers of newspapers before placing them in the ashes of the embers.

Nowadays, I wrap it in parchment paper and foil.

Ingredients

6	sausages
6	potatoes, scrubbed and cleaned
6	onions, peeled
	heavy foil paper

Method

Individually wrap sausages, potatoes and onions in separate sheets of foil paper. Place under hot ashes and cook for about an hour. (They are ready to serve when the aroma beckons you. ❖

Rita's Prosciutto Cotto

Serves 30

This is another old-fashioned recipe which has taken me five years of intermittent testing to perfect. It is absolutely delicious, hot or cold. Enjoy!

Ingredients

1	leg of pork approx 15 - 20 lbs
1/2	cup coarse salt
2	tsp hot pepper
1	tsp black pepper
1	Tbsp ground ginger
1/2	tsp mustard seed
3	Tbsp fennel seeds
1/2	tsp curry
20	juniper berries
1/2	cup gin
1/2	cup white wine for rinsing

Method

Place leg of pork in a large dish. Rub leg with salt. Add remaining ingredients and rub all over. Cover with clean plastic bag with a heavy weight of at least 20 lbs on top. Place in cold storage or wine cellar, turning once a day for three days. Rinse with white wine before baking.

Baking Dish Ingredients

4	Tbsp olive oil
5	garlic cloves
5	sprigs parsley
1/2	tsp fennel seeds
2	tsp tarragon
1	tsp savory
5	bay leaves
1/2	cup water
3	baking apples

Method

Preheat oven to 350° F. In a baking pan, combine the ingredients. Cover leg with foil and allow 1 hour for every 4 lbs. Remove foil half an hour before it is done.

Take leg of pork out of the oven after approx. 5 hours. Strain herbs and apples from the gravy. Slice pork and serve hot with gravy ladled over. Or serve cold with a pickled salad. ❖

Easter Bread
Recipe page 162

Cracked Wheat with Chick Peas and Pork

(Grano rotto con ceci e maiale)

Serves 6

Ingredients

2	cups cracked wheat
4	cups chick peas, cooked
1-1/2	lbs pork shank
2	garlic cloves, chopped
2	leeks, chopped
2	bay leaves
1/4	cup olive oil
	salt and pepper to taste

Method

Rinse pork with cold water. Place pork in a pot and cover with water. Let boil for 5 minutes. Drain and let cool. Rinse the cracked wheat. Put wheat in a pot and cover generously with water. Cover and simmer for 20-25 minutes, on low heat, or until cooked. Then put wheat aside for later use. In a larger pot (that will hold everything) place oil, leeks, chopped pork and bay leaves on medium heat. Turn until golden. Now, add tomatoes, cooked chickpeas and wheat. Shake pot, cover and simmer for 10-15 minutes. Salt and pepper to taste and serve. ❖

Cabbage and Beans

(Cavolo e fagioli)

Serves 6

Ingredients

1-1/2	lbs of kidney beans
1-1/2	lbs cabbage (approx. 1 small cabbage)
2	chopped garlic cloves
1	medium tomato, peeled and chopped
1/2	cup of fresh fennel, chopped
3	Tbsp of virgin olive oil
	salt and pepper to taste

Method

Wash beans and soak overnight in a pot, covered with plenty of water. The next day, place pot on stove at medium heat for 5 minutes. Finely chop cabbage and rinse with salt and water. Place cabbage on top of beans. Then, put fennel, garlic and tomato in the pot, and bring to boil Preheat oven at 250° F. Then, place ingredients in an oven-proof casserole with a lid and place in oven for 2-1/2 — 3 hours. Before serving, pour olive oil on top. Salt and pepper to taste. ❖

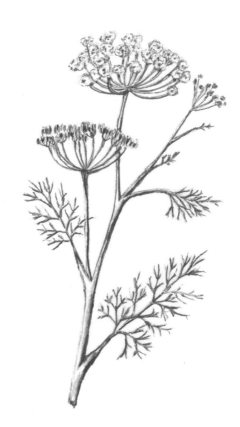

Blood Pudding

(Sanguinaccio)

Serves 12

Those of us who lived in the mountains took pride in raising our pigs for the Annual Garlic Fair. They were raised in special pens and put on a special diet that included bran mixed with water (drained from pasta or greens), boiled potatoes, fruit peel and leftover salad.

They were also fed boiled lupini which had been sweetened and dried. In fact, they were often fattened with chickpeas, acorns, chestnuts and figs.

When the pigs were slaughtered, the blood was collected for this Southern speciality. There were always variations in the way each household prepared their sanguinaccio, and that's why the recipe was coveted by both neighbours and friends.

This is my mother's recipe, which she refused to divulge for years, and was revealed only to me. The pudding was double-boiled in a copper pan over another pan full of water. Inside this other pan was placed a ceramic tile to keep the temperature constant and prevent the water from boiling.

We also used to buy pine cones as big as pineapples. We placed them close to the fire so the heat would open them up, revealing the black pine nuts inside. Within these pine nuts were the white ones we used for the pudding.

This was a special treat which my mother gave us but once a year. She would serve it with a fresh herbal tea.

Ingredients

1-3/4	pints pig's blood, strained
1-3/4	pints vino cotto
1/4	cup raisins
1/2	cup pine nuts
1/4	tsp cinnamon, freshly ground
2	Tbsp orange peel
4	oz Swiss chocolate

Method

Place the blood and the vino cotto in a double boiler. Cook very slowly over very low heat for two hours. Do not let it boil.

Keep stirring until it becomes very creamy before adding the remaining ingredients. Remove from heat when it has acquired the texture of molasses and the colour of burnt burgundy.   ❖

Scauille

This sweet is so named because it looks like steps. This is another traditional recipe which is served at Christmas.

Ingredients

9	egg yolks
1	egg
2	Tbsp sugar
2	Tbsp lard
1	Tbsp vanilla
2	Tbsp baking powder
2	Tbsp anise liqueur
2	cups all-purpose flour
2	bay leaves
	enough oil for frying

Method

Beat egg yolks, egg, sugar and vanilla.

Sift baking powder and flour. Pour onto rolling board. Make a well in the centre. Add the egg mixture, lard and liqueur. With a rotating motion, mix well. Knead for 2-3 minutes until shiny. Place in a buttered bowl and let it rest for 10 minutes.

Take a piece of dough. Roll it about 10" x 1/4". Place the dough on the tip of the handle of a wooden spoon. Turn spoon over the dough 3 times. Press the spoon against the rolling board. Flip to the other side and press again. Pull out the dough from the spoon.

Roll the rest of the dough in various designs.

Put enough oil in a pan for deep frying. Add bay leaves. When the oil is hot, drop scauille in. Turn once when they are golden and remove with a slotted spoon. Set aside to cool.

Glazing

2	cups honey
	grated rind of 1 orange
1/4	cup anise liqueur

In a pan, bring to a boil all the glazing ingredients. When it turns deep golden and bubbly, add scauille. Stir quickly and gently with a slotted spoon. Turn out onto a dish. ❖

Turdilli

Calabria is famous for its turdilli, another traditional offering at Christmas.

Ingredients

4	eggs
2	cups olive oil
1	cup Moscatello wine
	rind of 1 orange
1/2	tsp cinnamon
1/4	tsp cloves
4 1/4	cups all-purpose flour
1	tsp salt
2	bay leaves
	enough oil for frying

Method

In a pan, bring wine, orange rind, oil and Moscatello wine to boil. Turn heat off. Add flour at once, stirring with a wooden spoon until it is absorbed.

Add 1 egg at a time, stirring until they are all absorbed. Turn out onto floured board. Roll out into a foot-long piece. Cut into strips 2" long.

Press lightly with tips of 2 fingers against a cheese grater and flip each piece quickly against it so that it curls and forms a little gondola. Place on cookie sheets lined with waxed paper.

Put enough oil in a pan for deep frying. Add bay leaves. When the oil is hot, drop turdilli in. Cook over low heat. When they turn a little dark, remove with a slotted spoon.

Place individually on a platter with absorbent paper to cool.

Use the same glazing as for scauille. ❖

Italian Turnovers

(Chianuille)

Serves 50

Ingredients

6	egg yolks
6	egg whites
1	cup butter
1	cup vino cotto or vermouth
1/2	tsp salt
2	Tbsp baking powder
1	Tbsp vanilla
5	cups all-purpose flour
1/2	cup coarse sugar for sprinkling

Method

This can be done the day before.

Beat egg yolks, butter and vino cotto together.

Sift baking powder, salt and flour together. Make a well in the centre. Add egg mixture. With a rotating motion, mix well. Knead for 2-3 minutes until shiny. Place in a buttered bowl and let it rest for 10 minutes or refrigerate until ready for use.

Roll out dough to 1/8" thickness onto a floured board. With a wine glass, cut into circles.

Use the same raisin filling as for Mrs. Gallucci's Christmas Cake or Pitta Imbrogliata. Place 1 tsp of filling in each circle. Flip over on 1 side. Crimp edges with a fork.

Place on cookie sheets lined with persimmon paper. Beat egg whites. Brush over the top and sprinkle with sugar.

Bake in a preheated oven at 350° F for 5 minutes. Turn heat down to 300° F and bake for another 5-8 minutes.

Hint: Invest in a freezer and oven-proof casserole dish with a lid for serving.

Mrs. Gallucci's Christmas Cake

(Pitta imbrogliata)

Makes 6 cakes

I remember this cake as a child. It's a very traditional Christmas cake which they make in the province of Cosenza. I searched for this recipe for years before Signora Gallucci kindly consented to show me how it's done. I give this cake to my Canadian friends, who all love it.

Raisin Filling

4	lbs sultana raisins, washed and dried
3/4	lb hazelnuts, finely chopped
1-1/2	lbs walnuts, finely chopped
3/4	lb almonds
3/4	cup honey
1	cup peach jam
1/4	cup anise liqueur

In a saucepan, combine all the ingredients. Cook over medium heat for 5-10 minutes until shiny and sticky. Set aside to cool.

The filling can also be done the day before.

Dough

3	envelopes yeast
3	Tbsp sugar
1	cup warm water (100° F)
8	eggs
1	lb sugar
1	tsp salt
4	Tbsp orange peel, grated
	juice of 2 oranges
1-1/4	cups Moscatello wine
1	lb lard
15	cups all-purpose flour
6	yards string

Method

Dissolve the sugar in warm water. Sprinkle yeast on top. Let stand for 10 minutes.

Warm Moscatello wine and lard in a saucepan until lard dissolves. Set aside to cool.

In a large bowl, beat eggs, orange peel and sugar together.

Add orange juice, salt and about 2 cups of flour, blending well.

Add the yeast and wine mixtures. Add the flour gradually until it is absorbed. Knead for 2-3 minutes until the dough is smooth. Place in a buttered dish and cover with a linen cloth for 1 hour. Take a piece of dough and form a circle 9" in diameter and 1/8" in thickness. Put aside for later use.

2	cups honey
1	Tbsp cinnamon
1/2	tsp cloves

Mix the 3 ingredients together in a bowl for later use.

I use a lasagna machine numbers 1-5. But you can roll the dough out with a rolling pin to make strips 3 ft long, 4" wide and 1/8" thick.

Drizzle 1 tsp honey mixture along the middle of each strip. Heap 4-5 Tbsp of the raisin filling continuously from one end of the strip to the other.

Fold the dough over the filling. Roll gently round to the end. Place on the circle of dough formed earlier. Tie with string.

Line cookie sheets with parchment paper. Place 2 cakes each on a cookie sheet. Cover with a linen cloth for 1 - 1-1/2 hours.

Bake in a preheated oven at 350° F for 15 minutes. Reduce heat to 300° F and cook for approx. 1/2 hour longer. Test dough with toothpick to ensure that it comes clean. Cool completely.

Glazing

2	cups honey
1/2	cup anise liqueur

Combine ingredients in a pan. Bring to boil until it turns dark and bubbly. Brush glazing over the 6 cakes. Cool.

Wrap in waxed paper. Rewrap in foil. They keep very well for 2-3 months. ❖

SOUPS

Canadian Soup
Pasta Saporita
Vegetable Soup
Chicken Soup
Barley and Squash Soup
Fish Soup
Early-Autumn Vegetable Soup
Fava Beans and Home-Made Pasta
Turkey Soup

Canadian Soup

(Brodo canadese)

Serves 6

This is a delicious soup which is a meal in itself, served with freshly-baked home-made bread.

Ingredients

3	veal shank
10	pints water
1	large chicken
2	cups butter squash
2	leeks, greens included, chopped
2	bay leaves
1	hot pepper
2	tomatoes
2	carrots, chopped
1	garlic clove
1	piece ginger about 1"
	salt to taste

Method

Trim fat off chicken and veal shank. Cover with cold water and leave for about an hour. Rinse off with cold water. Then in a large pot, bring 10 pints of water and meat to boil. Skim foam off. Cover half-way and simmer for an hour.

Add the remaining ingredients and simmer for half an hour. Remove meat and chop. Then return meat to soup. When the soup is boiling, grate pasta saporita into it. ❖

Pasta Saporita

Serves 6

This pasta can be used in any soup.

Ingredients

1	cup all-purpose flour
1	egg
2	Tbsp parsley, minced
1/2	cup parmiggiano cheese
2	Tbsp milk

Method

This can be done ahead of time, wrapped in waxed paper and refrigerated until ready for cooking.

Place flour in a dish. Make a well, add remaining ingredients. Knead with one hand until all the ingredients form a smooth ball.

With larger side of cheese grater (which is normally used for grating mozzarella), grate entire ball of dough into the soup as it is cooking. When the pasta floats to the top, it is ready to be served. ❖

Vegetable Soup

(Zuppa di vegetali)

Serves 6

Ingredients

2	carrots
2	onions
2	potatoes
1	zucchini
1	cup spinach or romaine lettuce
1/2	cup rice, or pasta
1	garlic clove
2	bay leaves
1	hot pepper
12	cups water
2	parsnips or celery, chopped
2	Tbsp butter or olive oil
1/2	cup parmiggiano cheese (Reggiano)

Method

Bring water to boil. Add all remaining ingredients and simmer until all the vegetables are cooked.

Alternatively, blend vegetables in a blender until creamy.

Just before serving, add butter or olive oil and parmiggiano. ❖

Chicken Soup

(Brodo di pollo)

Serves 10

Ingredients

1	chicken
13	cups water
1	leek
1	bay leaf
1	garlic clove
2	stalks celery
1	carrot
1	small piece ginger, peeled
1	small hot pepper
2	small ripe tomatoes
	hard ends of asparagus (optional)

Method

Cover the chicken with the water in a pan and bring to a complete boil. Skim fat off water with a strainer. Boil for at least half an hour.

Add remaining ingredients. Partially cover and cook for 20-25 minutes. Towards the end of the cooking time, add 1/2 tsp nutmeg or a little liqueur (optional), salt and pepper to taste.

Strain soup and set aside.

Striacciatella

6	eggs
2	Tbsp flour
2	cups parmiggiano cheese (Reggiano)
2	Tbsp minced parsley
1/4	tsp cinnamon

Beat all the ingredients in a bowl. Bring strained soup to boil and pour the egg mixture into the soup, stirring as you add. Turn heat off and serve. ❖

Barley and Squash Soup

(Zuppa di orzo e zucca)

Serves 6-8

Ingredients

12	cups water
1	cup barley
2	potatoes, peeled and diced
2	carrots, peeled and chopped
2	onions, chopped
2	garlic cloves, minced
2	cups squash, diced and peeled
2	sticks celery, chopped
2	Tbsp parsley
2	cups tightly packed spinach, chopped
1	tomato
1	Tbsp butter or olive oil
1	cup parmiggiano cheese (Reggiano)
	salt and pepper to taste

Method

Place barley in boiling water. Add all ingredients, except butter or oil. Lower heat, partially cover and simmer for 3/4 hour, or until barley is tender. Just before serving, add butter or oil. Add parmiggiano cheese to each serving, as desired. ❖

Fish Soup

(Zuppa di pesce)

This is a tasty variant of the vegetable soup.

Ingredients

1/2	lb cod or any other fish fillet
1/2	lb monkfish
1/2	cup white wine

Method

Make the Vegetable Soup before adding the fish.

Rinse fish with wine. Cut into pieces. Simmer in soup for 5 minutes before serving. ❖

Early-Autumn Vegetable Soup
(Zuppa d'autunno)

Serves 8

This soup is healthy and refreshing. You can make a larger quantity, refrigerate and serve it later for other meals.

Ingredients

12	cups water
10	stalks swiss chard
2	small zucchini, rinsed and diced
1	medium onion
4	potatoes, peeled and diced
6	tomatoes, rinsed and minced
1-1/2	lbs frozen lima beans
2	minced garlic cloves
1	oz olive oil
2	Tbsp minced parsley
	salt and pepper to taste

Method

Fill a large pot with 12 cups of water and bring to a boil. Wash and cut swiss chard into 1-1/2" pieces and place in water. Add lima beans and bring to a boil again. Then remove swiss chard and beans with a slotted spoon. Discard water and place oil in pot. Add remaining ingredients to the pot. Cover and let simmer for 45 minutes on medium heat. Salt and pepper to taste. ❖

Fava Beans and Home-Made Pasta
(Fave e pasta)

Serves 6

Ingredients

2	lbs fresh fava beans, shelled
3	green onions, chopped
2	garlic cloves, minced
4	Tbsp oil
3	Tbsp fresh mint or sweet basil
1	cup water
1	lb home made pasta

Method

If you are buying fresh fava beans, you need 6 lbs. of fava, which will be reduced to 2 lbs. shelled. Wash fava beans after shelling.

Combine fava beans, green onions, garlic, oil and fresh mint or basil.

Place in a pot. Add water and bring to a boil. Cover and simmer for 20-25 minutes or until done.

Cook pasta according to package directions. Drain and mix together before serving. ❖

Turkey Soup
(Brodo di Tacchino)

Serves 6

Ingredients

1	lb turkey meat
3	leeks, cleaned and chopped
2	tomatoes, ripe, peeled and de-seeded
2	celery stalks, cleaned and chopped
2	carrots, rinsed and chopped
5	juniper berries
5	large spinach leaves, rinsed and chopped
2	garlic cloves
3	minced sage leaves
4	Tbsp chopped parsley
15	cups water
	salt to taste

Method

Place water and turkey into a pot and bring to a boil. Skim the surface. Then place all of the ingredients into the pot except the parsley. Simmer for 2 hours. Remove the turkey meat and cut it up into small pieces. Place meat back into the pot. Add parsley and salt to taste and serve. ❖

Photograph by Liana Tumino

Pasta with Sweet Ocean Sauce
Recipe page 73

The Owl's Eggplant Sauce
Recipe page 56

SAUCES & PASTA

Minced Meat Sauce
Angela's Sauce
Rucola Sauce
Refreshing Herbal and Mushroom Sauce
Butterfly Pasta with Ricotta Sauce
Scallop Sauce
Smoked Salmon Sauce
Shrimp with Spring Sauce
Stuffed Artichoke Sauce
Silana Mushroom Sauce
Rigatoni with Vegetable Sauce
The Owl's Eggplant Sauce

Minced Meat Sauce

(Salsa de manzo tritato)

Serves 6-8

Ingredients

1	lb minced beef
1	onion, minced
1	hot pepper
1	cup white wine
6	Tbsp oil
2	garlic cloves, minced
6	fresh basil leaves
3	bay leaves
5	juniper berries
4	whole cloves
1	piece ginger root, 1"
1/4	tsp allspice
2	26-oz cans tomato
2	lbs rigatoni

Method

Combine meat, onion, pepper, wine, 3 Tbsp oil and all spices. Marinate for 2-3 hours in the refrigerator.

In a heavy pot, heat 3 Tbsp oil and meat mixture. Sauté for 5 minutes, stirring frequently. Add tomatoes and simmer for an hour, stirring occasionally.

Cook rigatoni according to package directions. Pour hot sauce over and serve. ❖

Angela's Sauce

(Salsa all'Angela)

Serves 6

This is a rich sauce which is served with linguine. It was devised by my friend Angela Cantoni, and is a favourite of my eldest son Riccardo.

Ingredients

2	oz butter
4	garlic cloves
1	lb mushrooms

8	white onions, chopped
1	cup dry white wine
1	cup parsley
	freshly ground salt and pepper to taste
2	lbs linguine

Method

Place butter, garlic, onions and mushrooms in a pot. Cook covered over low heat for 2 hours, stirring occasionally, until onions are creamy.

Uncover and add wine and cook for another 20 minutes.

Just before serving, add parsley, salt and pepper.

Serve with linguine, cooked according to package directions, sprinkled with parmiggiano cheese. ❖

Rucola Sauce

(Salsa alla rucola)

Serves 6

This is such a quick and easy-to-make recipe. By the time the water boils for your pasta, you would have finished making the sauce!

Ingredients

2	white onions, sliced
1	leek, white part only, sliced
1	lb oyster mushrooms, shredded
1/2	cup white wine
1	bunch rucola, washed and chopped
1	oz butter
2	oz oil
1	little hot pepper (optional)

Method

Put butter and oil in frying pan. Add onions, leek and hot pepper. Cook covered over low heat for about 5 minutes until the onions are cooked.

Add mushrooms and wine, shaking the pan until the wine evaporates. Add rucola. Turn off the heat. Add salt and pepper to taste.

Cook spaghetti or linguine according to package direction. Mix with sauce and sprinkle with parmiggiano or romano cheese. ❖

Refreshing Herbal and Mushroom Sauce

(Salsa all'erbette con funghi)

Serves 6

Ingredients

1	lb mushrooms sliced
20	stalks garlic chives, chopped
8	branches fresh caraway leaves
2	silver onions, finely sliced
1	peppercorn
2	Tbsp tomato sauce
1/2	cup olive oil
1/2	cup wine
2	lbs linguine

Method

Put the oil in a pan with onions and mushrooms. Sauté over high heat for 2-3 minutes, shaking the pan all the time. Add the wine. When it has evaporated, add the chives, caraway and the tomato sauce. Turn the heat off.

Cook linguine or any pasta according to package directions. Ladle sauce over pasta and enjoy. ❖

Butterfly Pasta with Ricotta Sauce

(Farfalle alla ricotta)

Serves 6-8

This is my youngest son Leonardo's favourite dish. My mother used to make this too, but hers was made with a tender ricotta made from goat or lamb's milk. I have made some adjustments, adding milk, butter and egg yolk to enrich it. This sauce can be made earlier in the day, covered, and refrigerated until it is ready for use.

Ingredients

2	fresh ricotta cheese
1	cup milk
1/4	tsp nutmeg
2	Tbsp parsley, chopped
1	Tbsp unsalted butter
1	egg yolk
2	lbs farfalle pasta
	salt to taste
	Parmiggiano cheese (optional)

Method

Combine all the ingredients except the pasta into a bowl. Mix well and add salt to taste.

Cook pasta "al dente" according to package directions. Drain the pasta in a colander and pour into a serving dish right away so the pasta does not dry. Pour the sauce over the pasta and mix well. Serve with parmiggiano cheese. ❖

Scallop Sauce

(Scallops Salsa)

Serves 6

Ingredients

1	lb scallops
1	lb mushrooms, cut fine
2	parsnips, grated
1	leek, white part only
3	ripe tomatoes, peeled, seeds taken out, chopped
1/2	cup white wine
1	Tbsp corn starch
2	oz butter
1	oz oil
2	Tbsp parsley, minced
2	lbs tagliatelle or linguine

Method

Put scallops in cold water with a little salt. Rinse and drain in a colander. Put butter and oil in frying pan. Add parsnips, leek and mushrooms over high heat for 2-3 minutes, shaking the pan. Add white wine, tomatoes and scallops. Keep shaking the pan for 2-3 minutes. Add corn starch, salt and pepper to taste. Turn heat off and add parsley.

Serve with home-made tagliatelle or linguine cooked according to package directions. ❖

Smoked Salmon Sauce

(Salsa di salmone affumicato)

Serves 12

This is a great sauce for parties. Beginning with an antipasto of smoked salmon decorated with caraway leaves, home-made pickles, capers, red onions and lemon, I go on to serve home-made dark rye bread with antipasto dip. I usually serve it with linguine or farfalle. My family always gives me a "10" for dinner, especially as Canadian salmon gives a full-bodied flavour to this sauce.

Ingredients

1/2	cup butter
3	green onions, white part only, chopped very fine
3	finely chopped garlic cloves
5	minced branches chervil
1/2	lb smoked salmon
4	cups milk
1	cup whipping cream
2	Tbsp flour
1/2	cup gin
*3	juniper berries
*4	fennel seeds
*2	black peppercorns
*5	chervil seeds
2	lbs linguine

*ground together to make 1/2 tsp

Method

In a non-stick pan, place butter, onions and garlic. Sauté over low heat until light golden. Add salmon and stir for 2-3 seconds.

Add gin and flour. Pour milk in and continue stirring until sauce thickens. Turn heat off before adding whipping cream.

Cook linguine according to package directions. Do not toss. Pour sauce over and serve. ❖

Shrimp with Spring Sauce

(Gamberi alla primavera)

Serves 6

Ingredients

2	lbs shrimp, cleaned
4	medium onions, chopped
2	parsnips, grated
5	garlic cloves, minced
1/2	tsp cayenne
1/2	tsp savory
1/2	cup white wine
1/4	tsp ginger
4	oz butter
	salt to taste
4	Tbsp parsley, minced
2	lbs farfalle (bow tie pasta)

Method

Rinse shrimps in cold water and place in colander. Add ginger, salt, cayenne and savory. Toss and set aside.

Melt butter in a saucepan. Add onions, garlic and parsnips. Cook covered over low heat till golden. Add wine.

Add shrimps. Stir and cook for 2-4 minutes until they turn orange. Turn off heat.

Prepare "bow tie pasta" according to package directions.

Pour shrimp sauce over pasta and sprinkle parsley over before serving. ❖

Stuffed Artichoke Sauce

(Carciofi ripieni)

Serves 6

Artichokes are both tasty and very nutritious. They have been found to be beneficial in the treatment of diabetes and rheumatism, gout and arteriosclerosis. They are also low in cholesterol and help to reduce cellulite.

In my own home town, we used to wash and dry the dark leaves and make a tea with it. We would pour a cup of boiling water over the leaves and let it stand for 15 minutes before drinking.

Ingredients

8	medium artichokes

Cleaning artichokes:

Clean artichokes by taking off all the dark leaves. Trim round the top and bottom so they can stand. Open the petals like a rose without breaking them. Scoop a little of the centre out. Put them in a large dish of water, with a slice of lemon inside the water. Take the artichokes out of the water and dry them with a paper towel.

Filling

1	egg, slightly beaten
1	lb ground veal
2	garlic cloves, chopped
2	Tbsp butter
1/2	cup white wine
1	green onion, chopped
1/2	cup parmiggiano cheese
4	tsp breadcrumbs
1	Tbsp dry savory leaves
1/2	tsp dry thyme leaves
1/2	tsp dry tarragon leaves
	salt and pepper to taste

Method

Melt the butter in a saucepan. Add veal, garlic and onions, mixing well. Brown the meat for a few minutes. Add wine, spices, breadcrumbs, salt and pepper to taste. Put aside to cool. Add the eggs and cheese. Mix well and spoon the mixture into each artichoke, placing it between the leaves.

Ingredients for Sauce

2	chopped onions
1/2	cup olive oil
4	cups tomato sauce
2	garlic cloves, chopped

Method

Use a large pan capable of holding 8 large artichokes. Put oil in pan, add onion and garlic. Place artichokes into pan in an upright position. Cover and simmer at low heat for about 2 minutes shaking the pan occasionally.

Take off the cover and add tomato sauce. Simmer for another 10-15 minutes until they are tender when pricked with a fork.

Cook bucatini according to package directions. Serve sauce ladled over bucatini and artichokes on the side. ❖

Silana Mushroom Sauce

(Salsa alla Silana)

Serves 6

This is one of my mother's recipes using the mushrooms which used to grow so plentifully in Sila. Here in Canada, I make this with dried European mushrooms. It owes its distinctive taste to the use of fresh onions and mushrooms, and home-made tagliatelle.

Ingredients

2	oz olive oil
4	garlic cloves
1	cup dry mushrooms, washed and soaked
4	white onions, chopped
1	cup dry white wine
1	cup parsley
	freshly ground salt and pepper to taste
1	cup goat cheese
2	lbs tagliatelle

Method

Place olive oil, garlic, onions and mushrooms in a wide frying pan. Sauté over high heat for about 5 to 7 minutes, always shaking the pan or until the onions turn blonde. Add wine. Turn the heat off.

Just before serving, add parsley, salt and pepper.

Serve with tagliatelle, boiled according to package directions. Serve with goat cheese. ❖

Rigatoni with Vegetable Sauce

(Cannarozze alla Don Michele)

Serves 8-10

Ingredients

1	eggplant, diced about 1-1/2" in length
15	mushrooms, quartered
4	hot banana peppers, de-seeded, cut into 1" rounds
6	medium artichokes
1	Tbsp lemon juice
30	green olives, pitted
6	ripe plum tomatoes, peeled and de-seeded
3	garlic cloves, chopped
1	Tbsp salt
1/2	cup olive oil
2	Tbsp minced basil
2	lbs rigatoni
	grated goat cheese or parmiggiano

Method

Remove hard leaves of fresh artichokes. Trim top and cover with cold water and lemon juice.

In a colander, place eggplants, mushrooms and peppers. Sprinkle with salt, toss and cover with a dish. Leave for 10-15 minutes. Drain and dry with absorbent paper towel.

In a skillet, add olive oil and artichokes. Cook covered for 3-4 minutes. Remove artichokes with a slotted spoon. In the same oil, fry eggplants, mushrooms, olives and hot peppers individually until lightly golden. Drain oil.

Add garlic and tomatoes to 2 oz of new oil. Fry for 3-4 minutes. Add fried vegetables. Shake the pan until everything is coated with the sauce. Add basil leaves and salt to taste.

Cook rigatoni according to package directions. Place on platter. Pour vegetables over. Serve with cheese. ❖

The Owl's Eggplant Sauce

(Melanzane al gufo)

Serves 6

This recipe is named after an owl I noticed sleeping in my garden every time I went to pick eggplants. It is actually a recipe from my mother-in-law, Concetta Bumbaca, and is a popular summer dish.

Ingredients

4	medium eggplants
1/2	cup olive oil
1	tsp salt
1	cup parmiggiano cheese

Wash and cut the eggplants into squares. Sprinkle with some salt and leave them for at least an hour. Squeeze them and fry them in hot oil till they turn golden. Remove with a slotted spoon and place in a dish. Sprinkle cheese on top. Put them aside.

Sauce

2	28-oz cans tomatoes
1/4	cup olive oil
2	white onions, chopped
3	garlic cloves, chopped
2	Tbsp parsley, chopped
2	Tbsp fresh savory, chopped
2	lbs spaghetti
	salt and pepper to taste

Method

In a pan, add the oil, garlic and onions. Simmer for a few seconds. Add the tomatoes. Bring to boil. Simmer for 20 minutes, stirring occasionally. Add the savory, parsley and salt to taste. Turn heat off. Put the eggplants in the sauce.

Boil the spaghetti according to package directions. Drain and ladle sauce over. ❖

VEGETABLES

Baked Stuffed Eggplant with Nuts
Eggplant Parmesan
Stuffed Eggplant
Eggplant with Mint Sauce
Zucchini with Mint Sauce
Zucchini Fritters
Drowned Broccoli
Wild Rice with Zucchini and Mushrooms
Fried Zucchini with Parmiggiano
Oyster Mushrooms and Artichokes
Curly Cabbage Rolls
Asparagus and Carrot Salad
Stuffed Tomatoes with Basil
Calabrian Rice
Brussels Sprouts
Boiled Potatoes and Green Bean Salad
Cauliflower and Tomato Salad
Peas and New Potatoes
Chick Peas
Baked Romano Beans
Federico's Coleslaw
Federico's Mustard Spice

Baked Stuffed Eggplant with Nuts

(Melanzane ripieni con noci)

Serves 7

This dish keeps very well. It can be frozen for later use.

Ingredients

7	little eggplants
3	Tbsp butter
1	leek, white part only
15	green olives, pits removed, chopped
1	parsnip, chopped
6	walnuts, chopped
1	Tbsp capers, washed, chopped
4	sprigs parsley, chopped
2	sprigs tarragon, chopped
5	leaves sage, chopped
2	sprigs hyssop, chopped
5	Tbsp breadcrumbs
7	Tbsp parmiggiano cheese
1	egg, slightly beaten

Method

Cut eggplants in half and blanch in boiling water until fork-tender. Drain in colander and cool. Using a spoon, remove the pulp without breaking the skin. Place skin on waxed paper or in a dish and grate parmiggiano over top. Set aside.

Chop pulp of eggplants. In a wide pan, add 2 Tbsp butter. Sauté eggplant pulp, leek, green olives, parsnips, walnuts, capers and herbs for 2-3 minutes. Cool, then add egg, cheese and breadcrumbs. Stir well. Stuff eggplant skins.

Butter baking dish with remaining Tbsp of butter.

Ingredients for Baking Dish

8	branches parsley
2	garlic cloves, minced

Place the above ingredients in baking dish. Add stuffed eggplants and sprinkle remaining parmiggiano over the top.

Bake in oven at 350° F for 1/2 an hour.

Eggplant Parmesan

(Melanzane alla parmiggiana)

Serves 6

Ingredients

6	eggplants
1	cup flour
1/2	cup olive oil
	salt to taste

Wash and cut the eggplants 1/2" thick lengthwise. Place them in a dish, sprinkle with salt and place a heavy weight on top for 2-3 hours. Squeeze them and dry out on absorbent paper towels. Coat eggplants with flour and fry quickly in hot oil on each side. Arrange individually on flat dish and set aside.

Sauce

2	28-oz cans Italian plum tomatoes
1	5-1/2-oz can tomato paste
2	Tbsp olive oil
2	white onions, chopped
3	garlic cloves, chopped
10	sprigs parsley, chopped
2	Tbsp fresh savory, chopped
	salt to taste

In a pan, add the oil, garlic and onions. Simmer for a few seconds. Add the tomatoes and tomato paste. Bring to boil. Simmer for 20 minutes, stirring occasionally. Add the savory, parsley and salt to taste. Turn heat off.

1	mozzarella cheese, grated
2	cups parmiggiano cheese, grated
1/2	cup breadcrumbs

In a lasagna dish, layer first some sauce and then the fried egg plant. Sprinkle with breadcrumbs, mozzarella and parmiggiano. Then top again with sauce. Continue layering in this manner until everything is finished. Sprinkle top layer with mozzarella and parmiggiano cheese.

Bake in oven at 350° F for 3/4 hour.

Stuffed Eggplant

(Melanzane alla Concetta)

Serves 8

This is my mother-in-law's recipe.

Ingredients

8	small eggplants

Method

Cut eggplants in half and blanch in boiling water until fork tender. Drain in colander and cool. Using a spoon, remove the pulp without breaking the skin. Place skin on waxed paper or in a dish and grate parmiggiano over top. Set aside.

Stuffing

8	eggplant pulp
1	green onion, white part only, chopped
1	garlic clove, minced
2	mushrooms chopped
1	Tbsp capers, washed, chopped
1	potato, peeled and grated
1	tomato, peeled and chopped
2	fresh artichoke hearts, chopped
2	oz white wine
1	cup oil
1	Tbsp dry basil
1	cup breadcrumbs
1	cup parmiggiano
2	eggs, slightly beaten
15	sprigs basil leaves for decoration
	salt and pepper to taste

In a large bowl, mix everything together except the oil and the basil leaves. Add more breadcrumbs if desired. Let rest for an hour.

Stuff into eggplant skins.

In a non-stick pan, add oil. Fry stuffed eggplant, stuffing side down for about 2-3 minutes before turning over. Turn 2 or 3 times until golden brown.

Place basil leaves on the bottom of a serving platter. Remove eggplants from pan with a slotted spoon. Place on a platter and grate parmiggiano over the top. ❖

Eggplant with Mint Sauce

(Melanzane con salsa di menta)

Serves 8-10

Ingredients

12	small dark eggplants
1	Tbsp salt
1	cup oil

Cut eggplants in half, lengthwise. Make 1/2" incisions in the length and width so that they look like squares.

Sprinkle with salt and put in a dish with a heavy weight on top. Leave for about an hour. Squeeze and dry on absorbent paper towels.

Pour enough oil into a frying pan for frying. When oil is hot, fry eggplants on both sides, turning quickly for about a second. Drain on absorbent paper towels.

Mint Sauce

1	cup fresh mint
1/2	cup tarragon vinegar
2	garlic cloves
2	Tbsp breadcrumbs
20	mint leaves
2	oz pine nuts

In a blender, blend first 3 ingredients for 1-2 seconds.

In a long serving dish, add the mint leaves. Sprinkle some breadcrumbs and 1 Tbsp of the blender mixture. Layer with eggplant. Place pine nuts in the grooves of the eggplant. Continue layering until everything is finished.

This also keeps covered in a deep dish refrigerated for up to a month. ❖

Zucchini with Mint Sauce

(Zucchini con salsa di menta)

Serves 6

This is my mother, Maria Gallo's recipe. It's a very refreshing summer dish which can be prepared ahead and served with barbecued meat or fish.

Ingredients

6	medium fresh zucchini, cut lengthwise
12	cups water
1	tsp salt
1/4	tsp nutmeg

Method

Cut zucchini in half lengthwise, and then half again, about 1" wide.

In a pot of boiling water with salt and nutmeg, blanch the zucchini. Remove with slotted spoon and place in a colander.

Dressing

2	Tbsp breadcrumbs
1/2	cup mint
1	oz olive oil
1	garlic clove
1/2	oz white wine vinegar

In a blender, place all ingredients except breadcrumbs. Blend for a minute until creamy.

Place zucchini in a serving dish. Sprinkle breadcrumbs over top. Spoon the sauce over and serve. ❖

Zucchini Fritters

(Frittelle di zucchini al basilico)

Serves 6

Ingredients

4	large zucchini, sliced thinly
1	Tbsp salt
1	cup oil
2	garlic cloves
1/2	cup parmiggiano for garnish

Batter

1/2	cup parmiggiano
1/2	cup milk
2	cups flour
4	eggs, slightly beaten
15	fresh basil leaves, chopped
2	fresh sage leaves, chopped
1	garlic clove, minced

Method

Place zucchini rounds in a dish and sprinkle with salt. Stir well. Weigh it down with a plate. Let stand for an hour. Drain.

Mix all batter ingredients together until slightly thick. Add zucchini to batter and mix well.

In a frying pan, heat oil with 2 garlic cloves. When hot, drop tablespoonfuls of zucchini batter 1/2" apart. When circle of zucchini batter is golden, turn. Remove with slotted spoon.

Place individually on long serving dish. Do not place on top of each other. Continue until zucchini batter is finished. Grate parmiggiano over.

Leave uncovered otherwise they will become mushy. Serve hot or cold. ❖

Drowned Broccoli

(Broccoli affogati)

Ingredients

2	bunches broccoli
1	oz wine
2	oz olive oil
3	garlic cloves
1/2	red pepper

Method

Peel stems and cut lengthwise. Trim florets. Rinse in water and salt. In a pan, add oil, garlic, wine and red pepper.

Add broccoli and cook covered over high heat until tender, shaking the pan occasionally. Cooking time is approximately 5-10 minutes. ❖

Wild Rice with Zucchini and Mushrooms

(Riso selvatico con zucchini e funghi)

Serves 10

Ingredients

4	cups wild rice, rinsed
3	Tbsp butter
1	zucchini, diced
10	mushrooms, sliced
1	onion, sliced
1	garlic clove, sliced
3	Tbsp golden raisins, rinsed
1/4	tsp nutmeg, freshly ground
1/4	tsp saffron
2	Tbsp fresh tarragon, cut
2	bay leaves
2	Tbsp almonds, toasted and ground
1/2	cup sweet vermouth

Method

Soak raisins in 1/2 cup of vermouth.

In a saucepan, place rice and bay leaves. Cover with water. Bring to boil for 1 minute. Turn heat off. Stir and leave covered for later use.

Place butter, onions and garlic in a pan. Add zucchini, rice, mushrooms and cook covered over medium heat for 5 minutes. Add vermouth and raisins. Turn heat off. The residual heat will cook the rice. About 3-4 minutes before serving, add nutmeg, saffron, tarragon and almonds. Serve with chicken or fish. ❖

Fried Zucchini with Parmiggiano

(Zucchini fritti con parmiggiano)

Serves 6

Ingredients

6	medium fresh zucchini, cut lengthwise
1-1/2	cups olive oil
1	Tbsp salt
2	Tbsp savory, minced
2	Tbsp parsley, minced

Method

Cut zucchini in half, and then half again, about 1" wide and long. Sprinkle with salt. Stir well. Weigh it down with a plate. Let stand for an hour.

In a frying pan, add olive oil. Fry zucchini lightly on each side till golden.

In a serving dish, sprinkle parmiggiano, savory and parsley over. Layer in the same manner until everything is finished. Serve hot or cold. ❖

Oyster Mushrooms and Artichokes

(Funghi e carciofi)

Serves 6

Ingredients

1	lb oyster mushrooms, cut lengthwise
10	artichokes
1	tsp lemon juice
4	Tbsp sweet butter
4	whites of onions, chopped
4	garlic cloves, minced
2	oz sweet white wine
2	Tbsp capers, washed and squeezed
5	branches parsley, chopped
1	ripe tomato, peeled, de-seeded, chopped
	salt and pepper to taste

Method

Remove dark leaves of artichokes. Quarter and place in water with lemon juice.

Place butter in a frying pan. Add artichokes, onions and garlic. Cook over high heat, stirring constantly for 2-3 minutes.

Lower heat, add wine and cover for 5 minutes. Uncover. Add oyster mushrooms and shake pan. Add capers, parsley, tomato, salt and pepper. Shake pan. Turn off heat and remove to serving dish. ❖

Curly Cabbage Rolls

(Avvoltini di verza)

Serves 12

This is one dish you can make ahead and freeze for later use. I add some baking soda to the curly cabbage to retain its green colour.

Ingredients

1	head curly cabbage
1	tsp salt
1/4	tsp baking soda

Filling

2	lbs pork shoulder, freshly ground
1	lb rice (Vialone or Arborio), rinsed
3	medium green onions, minced
4	garlic cloves, minced
1	cup white wine
1/2	tsp nutmeg, freshly ground
1/4	tsp ginger, freshly ground
2	Tbsp fresh sweet basil
1	cup fontina cheese, grated
2	eggs, slightly beaten
10	basil leaves, minced
1/4	cup olive oil
4	Tbsp butter
4	cups chicken stock
	salt and pepper to taste

Method

Rinse cabbage and cut an X on the hard core. Place in a large pan stem downwards and cover with water. Bring to boil. Add baking soda and nutmeg.

After 5 minutes, remove and place under running cold water. Carefully separate leaves and place on waxed paper.

In a pan, add garlic, onions and meat to oil. Cook covered over medium heat for 2 minutes. Add rice, stirring for 2-3 minutes before adding wine. Add ginger, basil, fontina cheese, salt and pepper, stirring well. Turn heat off.

When it is cool, add eggs and mix well. Place about 2 tablespoons of the filling into each cabbage leaf. Take sides of cabbage and fold inwards. Take tip of leaf and roll towards the centre. Place individually in a casserole dish.

Continue rolling until everything is finished.

This should make enough for 2 casseroles. Cover casserole dishes with waxed paper. Top with foil. Then place in a plastic bag sealed with an elastic band. Label and date. This can freeze for up to 2 months.

Preheat oven to 300° F. When ready for use, take casserole dishes out of freezer. Bring to room temperature. Remove plastic bag, foil and waxed paper. Add 2 tablespoons of butter and 2 cups of stock to each dish. Cover with foil.

Bake for an hour or until done.

Asparagus and Carrot Salad

(Insalata di carote e asparaci)

Serves 6

Ingredients

2	bunches asparagus
2	horse carrots
1	Tbsp salt

Method

Wash, but do not peel carrots. Place them in a pot and cover with water. Cook until fork-tender. Cool. Peel skin off and cut lengthwise.

Cut off hard parts of asparagus. Place in cold water with salt. Let stand for a few minutes. Rinse and tie with string.

Place asparagus tips up in a pot. Make sure water reaches only 1/2 way up asparagus. Bring to boil for 2-3 minutes. Turn heat off. Untie asparagus and leave in water for 2 minutes. Drain.

Sauce

	juice of 1 lemon
1/4	cup olive oil
1	garlic clove
4	sprigs parsley
2	Tbsp white vinegar
	salt to taste

Method

Place all ingredients in a blender. Blend for a few seconds.

Arrange carrots and asparagus in a long serving dish. Pour sauce over. Mix and serve. ❖

Stuffed Tomatoes with Basil

(Pomidoro ripieni al basilico)

Serves 8

This is another easy-to-make dish which you can prepare in the morning and cook at night. You can serve it hot or cold. It is excellent as a summer dish or as a side dish.

Ingredients

8	medium tomatoes, not too ripe
8	Tbsp Italian rice
2	Tbsp fresh basil, chopped
2	garlic cloves
1/4	tsp nutmeg, freshly ground
1	cup mozzarella
	salt and pepper to taste
1/4	oz butter
10	leaves basil
2	Tbsp olive oil

Method

Rinse tomatoes and drain in a colander. Place rice in a dish, rinse with cold water and drain. Place dish under the colander to catch tomato juice.

Cut off the tops of the tomatoes. Take out the tomato pulp with a spoon. Place tomatoes in a dish, with tops. Squeeze pulp with your hands.

Add basil, nutmeg, mozzarella, oil, salt and pepper to the rice. Mix well.

Fill tomatoes 3/4 full. Cap tomatoes with the tops. Butter pan and add 10 leaves of basil. Bake in a non-stick pan in the oven at 350° F for 1/2 hour or until rice is tender. ❖

Calabrian Rice

(Risotto calabrese)

Serves 6

Ingredients

3	cups Italian rice (Vialone or Arborio)
1/2	tsp saffron
2	Tbsp oil
6	cups water
2	cups butter squash, diced
1/2	cup pecorino cheese
	salt to taste

Method

In a pot, bring all ingredients except the saffron to boil. Stir and simmer for 3 minutes. Turn off heat. Leave pot covered on burner for 20-25 minutes. The residual heat will cook the rice. About 3-4 minutes before serving, add saffron. Stir until the rice and squash are an even yellow in colour. Serve with pecorino cheese.

Hint: When cooking Italian rice, double the amount of water or stock per cup of rice. ❖

Brussels Sprouts

(Cavolini de Bruxelles)

Serves 6

Ingredients

1-1/2	lbs brussels sprouts
1	Tbsp salt
3	garlic cloves, minced
2	leeks, chopped
2	bay leaves
5	cherry tomatoes
2	Tbsp pine nuts, lightly toasted
3	stalks fennel heads, chopped
1/4	cup olive oil
1	oz white wine
1/4	tsp cayenne
	salt to taste

Method

Remove the dark leaves of the brussels sprouts and soak in a bowl of water with salt. Mark an X on the bottom of each brussels sprout. Add to dish of water.

In a pan, add olive oil, garlic, fennel, leeks, bay leaves and brussels sprout leaves. Cook covered for 1 minute over high heat, shaking the pan.

Add sprouts and wine. Cook covered for 6-8 minutes. Add pine nuts and tomatoes, salt and cayenne. Turn off heat. Keep covered and ready to serve. ❖

Boiled Potatoes and Green Bean Salad

(Insalata di patate bollite con fagiolini verdi)

Ingredients

6	potatoes, scrubbed
1	lb green beans, washed and cleaned

Method

Add green beans to a pot of boiling water and cook until fork-tender. Remove with a slotted spoon. In the same water, add potatoes and cook until fork-tender. Remove and dice potatoes into quarters.

Mix potatoes and green beans.

Hot Dressing

2	Tbsp melted butter
15	sprigs parsley, chopped
	salt and pepper to taste

Mix well and spoon over potatoes and green beans which have been kept warm.

Cold Dressing

1	oz olive oil
15	sprigs parsley, chopped
1/2	oz white vinegar
1	red onion, sliced in rings
	salt and pepper to taste

Place all dressing ingredients in a jar and shake well. Just before serving, spoon over potatoes and green beans. ❖

Cauliflower and Tomato Salad

(Insalata di cavolfiore e pomidoro)

Salad Ingredients

1	head cauliflower
1	red onion, cut in rings
2	tomatoes, not too ripe, cut into large pieces

Dressing

1	tsp oregano
1	oz olive oil
1/4	tsp cayenne
10	sprigs parsley
2	Tbsp raspberry vinegar
	salt and pepper to taste

Method

Wash cauliflower and place in a pot covered with water. Boil for 2-3 minutes. Cool. Break into large pieces. Place in a salad bowl with onion rings and tomato.

Place oil, cayenne, oregano, vinegar, salt and pepper to taste in a jar. Shake well and pour over salad. Sprinkle parsley before serving. ❖

Peas and New Potatoes

(Piselli e patatine novelle)

Serves 6

I like this dish with sweet potatoes or new potatoes. Sometimes, I even use turnips as a substitute.

Ingredients

2	lbs peas, freshly shelled
1	lb new potatoes, scrubbed and quartered
2	green onions
2	garlic cloves
2	oz butter
2	Tbsp fresh mint

Method

Place freshly shelled peas and potatoes in cold water.

Put butter and onions in a pan. Take peas and potatoes out of water, and add to pan. Cook covered over medium heat for 10-15 minutes, shaking the pan occasionally. Add salt and pepper to taste.

Just before serving, sprinkle fresh mint over top.

Chick Peas
(Ceci con limone)

This dish brings back memories of my childhood. My grandmother used to make this dish. She used to dip a piece of bread in the chick peas and give it to us. It made a nice snack especially when we came in from the cold after school.

Chick peas are very healthy and can be served with polenta, salads, pasta or rice. They can also be made ahead of time and refrigerated.

Ingredients

1	lb chick peas
6	cups water
1/4	tsp baking soda
1	piece ginger (about 1")
2	bay leaves

Method

The trick to cooking chick peas is to rinse them well under running water and soak them in water of the same temperature overnight. Then you cook with the same water it was soaked in. Add 1/4 tsp of baking soda before cooking. Always use a wooden spoon. Do not use a metal spoon.

The next day, preheat oven to 250° F. Boil chick peas in pot for 5 minutes. Place in the oven and cook covered for 3 hours. Then mix.

	juice of 1 lemon
4	Tbsp olive oil
10	branches parsley, chopped

When chick peas are cooked, pour mixture over. Stir and serve. ❖

Baked Romano Beans
(Fagioli romani al forno)

I cook all kinds of beans this way, and it's my sons' favourite dish. I usually prepare it in the morning at the same time that I'm making coffee, and leave it in the oven to cook with the timer on. When I return from work it's ready to be served.

Ingredients

1-1/2	lbs romano beans

Rinse romano beans and cover with enough water. Bring to boil in a large pan.

1	onion, chopped
2	garlic cloves
2	tomatoes
1	stalk celery
1	bay leaf
1	piece ginger (1") peeled

Method

Preheat oven to 250° F.

Place all ingredients in the bottom of a casserole dish. Add boiled beans and water to the casserole.

Bake covered for 5 hours.

Add a little olio santo to the top and stir. Serve with multi-grain bread and a pickled salad. ❖

Federico's Coleslaw

Serves 12

My husband Federico loves to entertain and there is nothing he likes better than to toss up a refreshing coleslaw, which goes incredibly well with his barbecues.

Ingredients

1	medium cabbage
1	small red cabbage
1	red onion
1	garlic clove
1/2	cup fresh mint, chopped
1	Tbsp fresh tarragon, chopped
2	tsp Federico's Mustard Spice
2	oz olive oil
	juice of 1/2 lemon
1	oz raspberry vinegar
	salt to taste

Method

This may be prepared 2 hours before serving.

Slice cabbage with salami machine or cut very fine. Soak in a bowl of cold water with 1 Tbsp salt. Drain well. Place in a bowl. Add the other ingredients. Mix well. Enjoy. ❖

Federico's Mustard Spice

This is a very special spice devised by my husband Federico. It is especially good for barbecues and imparts a distinctive flavour to the meal.

Ingredients

1	Tbsp peppercorns
1	Tbsp juniper berries
1	tsp mustard seeds
1	tsp fennel
1/2	tsp allspice
1/2	tsp red pepper
1/2	tsp cumin
1/2	tsp chervil

Method

Grind very finely in a pepper mill.

Baked Stuffed Eggplant with Nuts
Recipe page 58

Eggplant with Mint Sauce
Recipe page 59

Rice and Spinach
Recipe page 143

SEAFOOD

Swordfish Basil Sauce
Swordfish on Embers
Crab and Shrimp Salad
Sweet Ocean Sauce
Shrimp with Lemon Grass
Canadian Salmon with Fresh Chervil Sauce
Fresh Salmon Sauce
British Columbia Fresh Salmon
Fort Myers Stingray
Lobster Tail Barbecue
B.B.Q. Codfish
Fried Cod with Spicy Onion Rings
Cod with Cabbage
Mr. Rossi's Smelts
Seafood Salad
Herring Roe
Boston Blue Fillet

Swordfish Basil Sauce

(Salsa di pesce spada con basilico)

Serves 4

Ingredients

1	lb fresh swordfish, sliced 1/4" thick
1	cup white wine
2	fresh white onions, chopped
3	garlic cloves, minced
1/2	cup fresh basil, chopped
4	fresh Italian plum tomatoes, chopped
1/4	cup olive oil
1	cherry red pepper, de-seeded, thinly sliced
	salt to taste
2	lbs linguine or spaghetti

Method

Pour 1/2 cup of wine over swordfish and let stand for later use.

In a wide frying pan, add oil, garlic, red pepper and onions. Cover for 2-3 minutes over low heat. Add wine and tomatoes. Cook covered for an additional 2-3 minutes. Uncover, add swordfish, basil and salt to taste. Cook for a minute or so until swordfish whitens.

Boil linguine or spaghetti according to package directions.

Pour swordfish sauce over and serve.

Swordfish on Embers

(Pesce spada alla brace)

Serves 4

Swordfish is a speciality in the province of Reggio. Nobody does Pesce Spada like they do there. My husband and I were driving through the town of Roccella, when we discussed bringing some freshly-cut swordfish back to my brother, in my home town.

We thought it impossible for the fish to remain fresh over the 4-hour journey, particularly since it was a sweltering hot day. But an elderly gentleman, who overheard our conversation, told me to buy some romaine lettuce and wrap the swordfish in the lettuce.

He said we could travel for 12 hours and that the fish would still keep fresh. I did precisely that. By the time we got back to Rogliano, sure enough, the fish was perfect. That's when we decided to cook it the old-fashioned way, over the embers in our fire-place.

Ingredients

1	lb swordfish, sliced into 4 pieces, 1/4" thick
1	cup wine
3	sprigs fresh oregano
1	Tbsp olive oil
1/2	garlic clove, squeezed
	salt to taste

Method

Pour 1/2 cup wine over swordfish. Let stand for later use.

Chop two sprigs of fresh oregano. In a dish, add a pinch of oregano, oil, garlic and wine.

Place two bricks on either side of the embers with a grill over bricks. Drain liquid from fish, then cook 1 minute on each side.

Remove fish onto a serving dish. With other sprig of fresh oregano, brush fish with oregano, oil, garlic and wine mixture.

Serve and enjoy!

Crab and Shrimp Salad

(Insalata di granchio e gamberi)

Serves 4

Ingredients

1	lb crab meat
2	lbs medium shrimp, de-veined
1	cup white wine
4	cups water
1/2	cup parsley
1/4	cup pine nuts
2	Tbsp olive oil
1	Tbsp raspberry vinegar
	juice of half a lemon
1	small garlic clove
	salt and pepper to taste

Method

In a pot, pour the wine and water. Bring to a boil. Add shrimp, boil for 1 minute, or until they turn orange. Drain and cool.

Place remaining ingredients, except crab and shrimp, in a blender. Blend until creamy. Place the crab meat and shrimp in a salad bowl. Pour the sauce over and mix well. Refrigerate until ready to serve. ❖

Sweet Ocean Sauce

(Salsa di pesce misto)

Serves 6

Ingredients

1	lb scallops
1	lb shrimp, de-veined
1	lb squid, cut into circles
1/2	cup gin
3	large onions, thinly sliced
3	garlic cloves, minced
3	bay leaves
1/4	cup butter
1/4	cup olive oil
2	Tbsp parsley, minced
15	cherry tomatoes
2	lbs fettucine

Method

Pour 1/4 gin over scallops, shrimp and squid and let stand for later use.

Put onions, garlic, oil and butter in a large frying pan. Cook, covered for 5 minutes until light blond.

Add 1/4 cup gin, scallops, shrimp and squid. Shake the pan until they turn opaque. Do not overcook.

Turn heat off. Add cherry tomatoes and parsley, keep covered until ready for use.

Boil fettucine according to package directions.

Pour sauce over fettucine and serve.

Shrimp with Lemon Grass

(Gamberi con erba limone)

Serves 8-10

Ingredients

2	lbs shrimp, washed and de-veined
*1	lemon grass plant, chop only tender leaves
6	juniper berries
1/2	Tbsp fennel seed, ground
10	sprigs fresh parsley
1	cup maraschino cherry liqueur
2	Tbsp breadcrumbs
2	Tbsp olive oil
2	garlic cloves, minced
	juice of 1/2 lemon
2	Tbsp unsalted butter
	salt to taste

Method

In a large bowl, combine all ingredients except the butter. Marinate refrigerated for at least an hour.

Sauté in butter over very high heat in a large pan for 5 minutes. Once they turn pink, they are ready.

Serve hot as a cocktail or as a main course.

*Lemon grass available at Chinese Supermarkets.

Canadian Salmon with Fresh Chervil Sauce

(Salmone Canadese con salsa di cerfoglio)

Serves 6

Ingredients

6	salmon steaks cut 1" thick
1/2	cup Asti Spumante
4	Tbsp fresh chervil, minced
4	sprigs caraway
1	Tbsp garlic chives, sliced very fine
2	Tbsp butter, melted
1/4	tsp white pepper
	salt to taste

Method

In a bowl, mix all ingredients except the salmon steaks and caraway.

Grill salmon steaks over very hot barbecue. Cook for 2-3 minutes on each side to your liking. Do not overcook.

Place sprigs of caraway in the bottom of a serving dish. Place salmon steaks over. Pour sauce over and serve with cooked peas and new potatoes. ❖

Fresh Salmon Sauce

(Salsa di salmone fresco)

Serves 6

Ingredients

4	fresh salmon steaks
1/4	cup olive oil
2	garlic cloves, minced
1	large silver onion
1/2	cup white wine
6	ripe tomatoes, peeled and mashed
6	fresh basil leaves, chopped
1	Tbsp fresh hyssop, chopped
1	Tbsp fresh savory, chopped
2	Tbsp fresh tarragon, chopped
1	lb bucatini

Method

In a medium pot, place oil, garlic and onion. Cover and cook for 2-3 minutes. Add wine and tomatoes. Cook covered for another 5 minutes. Add salmon and cook uncovered for 3-4 minutes until salmon turns opaque. Place salmon in a dish, discard the skin and bones. Flake the salmon and put it back into the pot for another 2 minutes. Add herbs.

Cook bucatini according to package directions. Serve with salmon sauce. ❖

British Columbia Fresh Salmon

(Salmone fresco della Columbia Britannica)

Serves 10

Ingredients

6	lbs salmon
2	branches tarragon
4	branches fresh caraway
1/2	cup verdicchio (wine)
2	Tbsp butter, melted
1	cooking onion, sliced
2	bay leaves
20	sprigs of parsley for garnish
2	lemons for garnish
	salt and pepper to taste

Method

In a large roasting pan with a rack, place 4 cups of water, bay leaves and onions. Place one branch of tarragon and 2 branches of caraway on top of the rack.

Rinse the fish with the verdicchio. Brush the fish with the butter, inside and out. Place on the rack and put the tarragon and caraway over the fish.

Cover the pan with foil. Bake in the oven at 400° F for 10 minutes, then reduce to 350° F for the remainder of the cooking time. Allow 20 minutes cooking time for each pound of fish.

Debone and serve in a large dish. Garnish with parsley and lemon wedges. ❖

Fort Myers Stingray

(Raia alla Fort Myers)

Serves 6

On a trip to Fort Myers, my brother Tony caught such a large stingray, that it was enough to feed our 3 families for 3 days! This is easily my most popular recipe for stingray.

Ingredients

3	lbs stingray, cut into 2" lengths
1	cup white wine
1/4	tsp fresh ginger, grated
6	leaves sage, minced
1/4	tsp paprika
3	garlic cloves, minced
	salt and pepper, freshly ground
2	Tbsp cornmeal
1	cup all-purpose flour
4	bay leaves
	oil for frying
4	parsley branches, minced

Method

In a dish, place the fish and all herbs (except the bay leaves and parsley). Add wine, pepper and salt. Marinate for an hour.

Transfer to colander and drain all juices. Sprinkle cornmeal on fish. Turn fish, then dip into flour. Place fish individually on a long piece of wax paper. Do not overlap.

Put oil and bay leaves into a frying pan. Fry fish until golden. Remove with a slotted spoon and drain on absorbent paper towel.

Place parsley at bottom of serving dish, then add fried fish and decorate with lemon wedges and serve. ❖

Lobster Tail Barbecue

(Aragosta alla brace)

Serves 6

Ingredients

6	lobster tails, rinsed

1	garlic clove, minced very fine
1	oz white wine
3	Tbsp parsley
2	Tbsp olive oil
1/4	tsp Federico's Mustard Spice
	juice of 1 lemon

Method

In a dish, mix all ingredients except the lobster tails. Cut through the middle of the inside shell of lobster tails. Barbecue for 3-5 minutes until shells turn orange.

Place lobster tails in a serving dish. Pour lemon mixture over top. ❖

B.B.Q. Cod Fish

(Baccalà alla griglia)

Serves 4

Ingredients

1-1/2	lbs of cod
1	red onion cut in rounds
1/2	cup white vinegar
2	Tbsp olive oil
1	Tbsp capers (rinsed and squeezed)
	juice of one garlic clove
	juice of half a lemon
2	Tbsp parsley, minced
2	medium tomatoes, cut in wedges
	salt and pepper to taste

Method

In a dish, place the white vinegar and the onion rounds. Let stand for half an hour. Drain and add the lemon juice, garlic juice, capers, oil and parsley.

Cook the fish on the B.B.Q. for 3-5 minutes. Flip over and continue cooking for another 3-5 minutes. Place the fish on a serving dish. Add salt and pepper to taste. Pour sauce over and garnish with the tomatoes. ❖

Fried Cod with Spicy Onion Rings

(Baccalà fritto con contorno di cipolle piccanti)

Serves 4

Ingredients

1	lb fresh codfish, cut into squares
3	eggs
1	tsp salt
1/4	tsp black pepper
1	cup breadcrumbs
6	medium onions, sliced
2	cups water
2	cups white vinegar
4	medium hot peppers, washed and carefully dried

Method

Beat eggs, salt and pepper. Place cod in egg mixture and leave for 1/2 an hour. Coat cod pieces in breadcrumbs. Place separately on wax paper. Do not overlap.

In a large frying pan, heat olive oil. Add cod pieces and fry until brown on both sides, remove with a slotted spoon and place on a platter.

Bring water, vinegar and salt to boil.

Separate onion slices into rings. Boil for 3 minutes. Remove with a slotted spoon.

Arrange onions on a platter around the cod in a decorative manner.

If used as a delicious antipasto, it provides 8 servings instead. ❖

Cod with Cabbage

(Baccalà con cavolo verza)

Serves 6

This dish can be made with either fresh or dried cod. If using dried cod, soak in water for a few days. Change the water 4-5 times a day until spongy to the touch. Squeeze each piece and dry with an absorbent paper towel.

Ingredients

1	lb fresh or dried cod
1	tsp salt (if using fresh cod)
1/4	cup olive oil
4	onions, chopped
1	hot pepper
1/2	head cabbage
1/4	cup white wine
1/4	tsp pepper
4	sprigs fresh parsley

Method

Heat oil in a large frying pan. Sauté onions and hot pepper for 1 minute. Remove.

Add cod and sauté on both sides until golden. Remove.

Add cabbage, wine and pepper. Cover and simmer gently for 5 minutes. Add cod, onions and pepper and cook for 10 minutes.

Place in a serving dish. Garnish with parsley. Serve with steamed rice. ❖

Mr. Rossi's Smelts
(Eperlano alla Rossi)

Serves 8-10

Every year, my neighbour Mr. Rossi goes fishing. On a number of occasions, he has brought back smelts, which I have cooked. This recipe is a particular favourite of my three children.

Ingredients

2	lbs smelts, cleaned, heads removed
4	leaves chervil, chopped
5	leaves tarragon
3	green onions, whites only, chopped
2	garlic cloves, minced
1/2	cup white wine
5	hot peppers
	salt to taste
1/4	tsp cayenne
1/2	tsp paprika
2	Tbsp cornmeal
1	cup all-purpose flour
2	cups olive oil
4	branches parsley, washed and dried

Method

Clean smelts, remove heads and intestines. Place smelts, wine and herbs in a dish. Sprinkle with cornmeal.

An hour before serving, drain smelts in a colander, shaking away excess liquid.

Cover the counter with waxed paper and add flour. Coat each smelt with flour.

Pour enough oil into a frying pan for deep frying. Fry smelts in hot oil on both sides until golden. Remove with a slotted spoon and drain on absorbent paper towel.

If you find that the oil darkens when you still have quite a few more fish to fry, drain away and add fresh oil to the frying pan.

Fry hot peppers and branches of parsley for a few seconds. Remove and drain on absorbent paper towel.

Arrange fried parsley, smelts and hot peppers in a serving dish. ❖

Seafood Salad
(Insalata di pesce misto)

Serves 6

This can be made a day ahead and served as an antipasto.

Ingredients

1	lb scallops
1	lb shrimp, de-veined
1	lb squid, cut into circles
1	lb octopus (about 3)
2	large onions
2	garlic cloves, minced
3	bay leaves
1/4	cup olive oil
2	Tbsp parsley, minced
2	Tbsp raspberry vinegar
1	Tbsp capers, rinsed out

Ingredients for Brine

4	cups water
1	cup white vinegar
1	garlic clove
1	bay leaf
1	hot pepper
1	Tbsp salt

Bring brine ingredients to boil. Add octopus and cook for 6-7 minutes until fork tender. Remove octopus with slotted spoon.

Add shrimps, squid and scallops and, when it comes to a boil, remove with a slotted spoon.

Add onions in the same brine and cook for 2 minutes. Remove.

Place octopus, shrimps, squid and scallops into a serving dish with the onions. Add olive oil, garlic, parsley, raspberry vinegar, capers and salt to taste.

Leave for an hour before serving. This can also be made ahead and refrigerated, covered, until ready for use. ❖

Herring Roe

(Aringa)

Serves 12

Ingredients

2-1/2	lbs herring roe
2	cups white wine
5	cups water
3	garlic cloves, unpeeled
3	bay leaves
2	peppercorns
1	sprig savory
5	juniper berries
1	fresh ginger, 1" peeled
1	sprig fresh tarragon
2	whole onions

Method

Place all ingredients except herring roe in a pan and cook covered over medium heat for 10 minutes. Add herring roe and continue cooking for another 10 minutes. Remove roe, onions and garlic onto a platter. Remove skin from garlic, mash with fork, and slice onions for use in the dressing.

Dressing

	juice of 2 lemons
2	Tbsp capers, washed and squeezed
2	Tbsp parsley, minced
3	Tbsp olive oil
1/2	tsp fresh savory
	salt and pepper to taste

In a bowl, mix all dressing ingredients with the sliced onions and mashed garlic. Pour over herring roe. Turn gently before serving. ❖

Boston Blue Fillet

(Filetto di Boston blue)

Serves 6

Ingredients

2	lbs Boston blue fillet
8	medium potatoes, peeled and cut in quarters
2	celery stalks
5	ripe, medium tomatoes, peeled and chopped
2	medium cooking onions, chopped
1	Tbsp parsley, chopped
2	garlic cloves, chopped
1	oz olive oil
1/2	cup white wine

Method

In a pot, place the oil, onions and garlic. Cover and cook for 2-3 minutes. Add tomatoes, potatoes and celery. Cover and cook on medium heat for 20-25 minutes, until potatoes are fork tender.

Cut fish in 3 inch pieces. Rinse with wine and place on top of the potatoes. Cover pan and simmer for 5 minutes, shaking the pan occasionally. Add salt and pepper to taste, sprinkle parsley over and serve. ❖

Rhubarb and Raspberry Flan
Recipe page 169

Baked Scallops
Recipe page 127

MEATS

Rabbit with Oyster Mushrooms and Artichokes
Donna Riccarda's Wild Rabbit
Rose's Chicken
Chicken with Marsala
Chicken with Vermouth and Wild Rice Stuffing
Goose with Pistachio
Veal Rump with Walnut and Onion Sauce
Veal Tenderloin
Veal Heart
Quails and Pasta
Calf Liver with Hot Sauce
Prime Roast
Silana Leg of Goat
Leg of Lamb with Mint
Hot Soup and Cold Dinner
Oxtail Stew with Potatoes
Tower Hamburgers
Ham with Brandied Cherries
Old-Fashioned Gelatine of Pig
Pork Chops with Juniper
Pork Tenderloin
Tri-Colour Paté
Meat Pie Crust
Rita's Special Spice

Rabbit with Oyster Mushrooms and Artichokes

(Coniglio con contorno di carciofi & funghi)

Ingredients

1	4-lbs rabbit
1	white onion
4	garlic cloves, minced
1	branch rosemary
1	branch mint
6	slices fresh ginger
1/2	cup white wine
1/2	cup oil
	freshly ground pepper and salt to taste
3/4	lb oyster mushrooms, hand-shredded
7	artichokes, cleaned and quartered
1	oz white vinegar

Method

Cut rabbit in pieces and completely cover in cold water. Add white vinegar and let stand for one hour before draining. Dry with absorbent paper towel.

Pour oil in a wide pan. Add rabbit, artichoke, onions and garlic. Cook covered for 10 minutes. Uncover, add white wine and allow liquid to evaporate. Add rosemary, mint and ginger as well as mushrooms, salt and pepper to taste. Cook for another 3 minutes. Turn heat off and serve.

Place rabbit pieces in serving dish, with artichokes and mushrooms in the middle. ❖

Donna Riccarda's Wild Rabbit

(Lepre alla Donna Riccarda)

Ingredients

1	3-lbs wild rabbit, cleaned and cut
	1 rabbit liver
1	cup red wine vinegar
4	bay leaves
5	juniper berries, crushed
1/2	cup olive oil
4	garlic cloves
1	red tomato, peeled and cut
1	Tbsp capers
2	Tbsp red raspberry vinegar
3	Tbsp parsley, chopped
	salt and pepper to taste

Method

Cut rabbit in pieces, place in bowl and completely cover with cold water. Add red vinegar and let stand for a few hours, then drain and towel dry.

Pour oil in pan, add bay leaves, garlic and rabbit. Cover for 15 minutes and cook over medium heat turning occasionally. Uncover and add juniper berries, tomato and capers. Keep stirring for 2-3 minutes.

Put the liver in the blender for a few minutes. When the rabbit is nicely browned, add liver, turning with a wooden spoon. Turn up the heat a little and sprinkle the raspberry vinegar over. Turn off and place in a serving dish. Decorate with chopped parsley. Serve with polenta, fried potatoes and a fresh green salad. ❖

Rose's Chicken

(Pollo alla Rose)

Serves 8

This is a Southern dish which my mother-in law used to cook. But it is dedicated to Rose, my Jamaican housekeeper, who was an excellent cook. We discovered that there were some similarities in Jamaican and Italian cooking. The difference was that, instead of olive oil and white wine, they used coconut oil and white rum.

Ingredients

3	Tbsp olive oil
2	chickens
2	onions, chopped
2	garlic cloves
1	small hot pepper (optional)
2	oz white wine
1/2	tsp thyme
3-4	branches parsley
5	juniper berries
2	tomatoes, cut into pieces
	salt and pepper to taste

Method

Wash and cut chicken into pieces. Place in a large bowl and add the rest of the ingredients. Marinate for a few hours, or in a refrigerator overnight.

Shake chicken pieces before cooking and place in a frying pan with enough oil. Fry each piece until golden.

Then place chicken in glass casserole and pour marinade over it. Bake at 350° for 1/2 hour. Turn chicken over and bake for an additional 15 minutes or until tender.

If you prefer, you may barbecue the chicken instead of frying it and then baking it in a casserole. In this case, cook marinade for 5 minutes and pour over chicken just before serving. ❖

Chicken with Marsala

(Pollo al marsala)

Serves 12

Ingredients

12	chicken legs, deboned and quartered
1/2	lb pork fillet, cubed
1/2	cup olive oil
1	leek, thinly sliced
2	shallots, thinly sliced
1	small onion, thinly sliced
4	garlic cloves, sliced
1	tsp grated fresh ginger, minced
1/2	cup marsala or white wine
1	Tbsp sifted cornstarch (optional)

Method

Debone chicken by cutting all the way around the ankle and around the top. Split through on the underside from the ankle to the top. Cut around the bone with a sharp knife.

Marinate the chicken and pork in a bowl and add 1/4 cup of marsala.

Combine all the ingredients in a wide frying pan before turning on the heat. Cook covered over high heat for 2-3 minutes. Uncover, stir the chicken and turn the heat down to medium.

Cook for 15 minutes. Add another 1/4 cup of marsala. If you want to thicken the sauce, add 1 Tbsp of sifted cornstarch.

Add

1	tsp tarragon
1/2	tsp sage
1/4	tsp turmeric
1/2	tsp curry powder
	salt and pepper to taste

Stir into sauce and spoon out into a serving dish. Serve with Saffron Rice. ❖

Chicken with Vermouth and Wild Rice Stuffing

(Pollo ripieno con riso selvatico)

Serves 8-10

Ingredients

2	roasting chickens (about 4 lbs each)
1/2	cup white vinegar
1/2	tsp cinnamon
1/4	tsp allspice
	salt and pepper to taste

Clean the chickens, rinse inside and out with vinegar. Sprinkle inside and outside with salt and pepper. Rub in well. Sprinkle with cinnamon and allspice. Rub again.

Stuffing

4	Tbsp butter
1	lb wild rice
1/2	cup water
2	cloves garlic, minced
4	onions, white parts only, minced
1	large cooking apple, chopped
4	walnuts, chopped
1/4	cup raisins, rinsed and soaked
1/2	cup dry vermouth
8	leaves romaine or spinach
2	leaves sage, crushed
1/2	Tbsp savory
1/4	tsp thyme
10	sprigs fresh parsley
	salt and pepper to taste

Method

Rinse wild rice, generously cover with water and bring to boil. Turn off burner and keep covered for later use.

Put butter, onions and garlic in a pan. Add rice, apples, walnuts, raisins and four chopped romaine leaves. Cook uncovered for 5 minutes, turning all the time.

Add herbs and salt and stir. Spoon the stuffing equally into the two chickens. Fold Romaine leaves so they form a natural net to keep the stuffing in.

Baking Dish Ingredients

10	cherry tomatoes
4	pieces fresh ginger root (about 1")
4	bay leaves
1/4	cup olive oil
1	branch sage
1	branch tarragon
1	branch savory
1	branch hyssop
1/2	cup dry vermouth

Preheat oven to 400° F.

Combine all baking dish ingredients except vermouth and make a bed for the chicken. Arrange chicken, breast-down, in the dish.

Cover and roast at 400° F for 10 minutes. Reduce heat to 375° F and continue roasting for 1 1/4 hours or until done. Halfway through cooking, turn the chickens breast side up, baste with the juice and continue baking.

Uncover chickens 10 to 15 minutes before they are done and let them brown. Take them out. Pour vermouth over the hot chickens.

Strain herbs, remove excess fat from juice.

In a serving dish, place the stuffing. Cut chickens into required portions and ladle juice over chicken. Serve with a nice green salad. ❖

Goose with Pistachio

(Oca al pistacchio)

Serves 10

Stock

	neck, feet, stomach and heart of goose
8	cups water
1	carrot
1	onion
1	clove garlic
1	tomato
1/2	tsp tarragon
1/2	tsp savory
1/2	tsp sage
2	bay leaves
2	sprigs parsley
	salt and pepper to taste

This can be cooked the day before. Rub stomach with 1 Tbsp of salt and rinse out. Place neck, feet, stomach and heart of goose in 8 cups of water.

Bring to a boil and skim foam off. Add the remaining ingredients and simmer for 1-1/2 hours.

After apportioning 3 cups of stock for the recipe, the remaining stock may be served as soup.

Ingredients

8	lb goose
1	lime, halved
2	tsp winter savory
2	Tbsp hyssop
	salt to taste

Stuffing

3	cups rice (Vialone or Arborio)
1/4	tsp saffron
1	parsnip, peeled and shredded
1	cup stock
1/2	cup pistachio, shelled
1/2	cup raisins, washed and soaked
1	cup white wine

	salt to taste
1	oz white wine for gravy

Roasting Pan Ingredients

2	cups stock
6	cherry tomatoes
4	cloves garlic
2	stalks lemon grass, cleaned, cut lengthwise
4	bay leaves
1	parsnip, cut lengthwise
10	sprigs parsley

Method

The night before, rub the goose all over with lime, savory, hyssop and salt on the inside and outside.

The following day, remove any visible fat. Place the goose and fat in a pan over medium heat. Add 1/2 cup white wine and brown the goose on both sides. Remove the goose and place in a dish.

In the same pan sauté rice, parsnip, raisins and pistachios for a few seconds before adding the stock and the remaining wine. When the liquid evaporates, add the saffron. Stir.

Preheat the oven to 350° F. Stuff the goose, and sew up cavity. Place roasting pan ingredients into pan. Place goose stomach down on roasting pan. Cover with foil and bake for 1 1/2 hours. Turn goose over and bake for another 1 1/2 hours.

To make the gravy, strain the dripping and add 1 oz white wine. Stir well. Skim additional fat off and save for later use. An option is to bake potatoes or cook with cabbage. ❖

Veal Rump with Walnut and Onion Sauce

(Girello di vitello con salsa di noci et cipolle)

Serves 6

Ingredients

1	veal rump (2-1/2 - 3 lbs)
4	large silver onions, sliced
1/2	cup white wine
3	garlic cloves, minced
1/2	tsp thyme
1/2	cup minced parsley
1/4	tsp cayenne
1/4	cup olive oil
6	walnuts
	salt and pepper to taste

Method

Shell walnuts and place in cold water for 1 hour. Remove from water, peel off dark skin and place in a mortar and pound to a paste. Place oil and veal rump in a pan, brown for approximately 3 minutes on high heat, constantly turning the rump. Then turn heat to medium and add wine, onions and garlic and cover. Let simmer for 1-1/2 hours turning the rump occasionally. When cooked, uncover and add parsley, walnut paste and salt to taste. Stir for one minute and remove from heat. Slice rump and place in a serving dish and top with its own sauce. (The sauce is enough to have a side dish such as steamed rice, cooked pasta or sliced boiled potatoes.) ❖

Veal Tenderloin

(Vitello alla fiamma)

Serves 6

Ingredients

2	veal tenderloin, cut 1 1/2"

Marinade

1/2	oz oil
2	garlic cloves
1/2	tsp rosemary
8	juniper berries
3	sprigs parsley
1	oz white wine
	salt and pepper to taste

Method

Blend marinade ingredients in a blender for 1/2 minute.

Place meat in a dish and pour the sauce over. Turn in sauce 2-3 times and cover. Marinate for about an hour before grilling over a barbecue for 2-3 minutes on each side. Do not overcook. ❖

Veal Heart

(Cuore di vitello alla delizia)

Serves 6

This was a quick, easy and absolutely delicious dinner I whipped up for special friends from Italy. Although it was done at short notice, the fact that they were still talking about it years later shows what a big impact it made.

Ingredients

1	big veal heart
14	large mushrooms, cleaned and sliced
2	ripe tomatoes, peeled and chopped
3	garlic cloves, minced
1/4	cup olive oil
2	sweet red peppers, washed and cut lengthwise
4	Tbsp parsley, minced
2	oz cognac
	salt and pepper to taste

Method

A day or two before, place the heart in a pot. Cover with water. Bring to boil and cook for about 1/2 hour or until fork tender. Drain and refrigerate.

Just before cooking, cut all the fat and hard muscles off. Cut into long strips.

In a non-stick frying pan, place oil, onion, garlic, pepper and mushrooms. Cook over high heat for 5-6 minutes, constantly turning with a wooden spoon.

Add the heart, tomatoes, salt and pepper. Continue cooking for another 5 minutes. Add cognac. Flambé. Add parsley. Turn off the heat. Cover until ready to serve. ❖

Quails and Pasta

(Quaglie e fusilli)

Serves 6

In my home town the quails were usually served with fusilli, a home-made pasta made by shaping it round the spindles that were often used in spinning silk.

Ingredients

1	fillet pork tenderloin, cut into small pieces
6	quails
2-1/2	oz olive oil
3	cloves garlic
2	green onions, whites only, chopped
2	oz white wine
4	sprigs parsley
1	sprigs rosemary
4	cups pureed tomatoes
	salt and pepper to taste
2	lbs fusilli
1	cup goat cheese

Method

Place oil in a frying pan. Add onions, garlic, pork tenderloin and quails. Cook over high heat for 5 minutes, turning constantly until golden. Lower heat and simmer for 10 minutes.

Add wine and herbs, salt and pepper. Cook for another 5 minutes. Remove quails and tomatoes. Cook for 10 minutes. Stir occasionally. Replace the quails in the sauce for another 5 minutes. Place quails in a serving dish.

In the meantime, cook fusilli according to package directions. Ladle sauce over fusilli. Sprinkle with goat cheese, as desired. ❖

Calf Liver with Hot Sauce

(Fegato con salsa piccante)

Serves 6

Ingredients

1/2	cup sweet vermouth
6	slices calf livers, 1/2" thick
4	Tbsp butter or oil
6	green onions, chopped
1	Tbsp capers, washed and drained
1	stalk celery, chopped
1	hot pepper, julienne
1/2	cup parsley, chopped
4	bay leaves
1/2	tsp sage
2	Tbsp breadcrumbs
	salt to taste

Method

In a dish, pour vermouth over liver and set aside.

Place butter or oil and all remaining ingredients except breadcrumbs in a frying pan. Stir and cook over medium heat for 5 minutes. Set aside to use as sauce.

Sauté liver and vermouth. Add breadcrumbs, salt and pepper and stir. Place liver in a serving dish and pour sauce over. Serve immediately. ❖

Prime Roast

(Filetto di manzo alla grappa)

Serves 10-12

Ingredients

5	lbs roast beef butt
3/4	cup grappa
5	garlic cloves
2	celery sticks
2	tomatoes, peeled
2	onions
1	bunch parsley
5	cloves
1/2	tsp rosemary
1/2	tsp black pepper, ground
4	bay leaves
4	sage leaves
1	Tbsp hyssop, chopped
	salt to taste
4	Tbsp olive oil

Method

Put roast in roasting pan and pour half of the grappa over it. Add all the remaining ingredients except the celery. Rub into the roast. Marinate for 12 hours or overnight. Turn roast over whenever possible.

Place celery sticks on the bottom of the roasting pan. Put roast on top. Preheat oven to 400° F. Place roast in oven for 10 minutes. Lower to 350° F. Allow 20 minutes per lb. Bake to your liking.

When done, take out of the oven. Add remaining grappa. Strain the juice from the roasting pan to make the gravy. Place in a saucepan and cook for about a minute until thick. Cut roast and pour gravy over top. ❖

Silana Leg of Goat

(Coscia di capretto alla Silana)

Serves 10

Sila is the plateau near our family home. On a clear day, you can see both sides of the ocean from the summit, and the view is simply breathtaking. Its resemblance to Muskoka in Canada is uncanny, with its three artificial lakes.

Sila is a popular tourist resort both in summer and winter. If you go at the right time, you can pick all kinds of different mushrooms. The last time we were there, we were treated to a simply scrumptious leg of goat barbecue and potato salad. The recipe for the leg of goat is one you should not miss if you go to Sila, and is reproduced below.

Ingredients

1	leg of goat
1	cup dry white wine
1	cup parsley
4	garlic cloves
1/2	tsp freshly ground black pepper
1/2	tsp cayenne
2	Tbsp oil
1	Tbsp oregano

Method

Debone the leg of goat. Blend the rest of the ingredients in a blender for one minute. Place the leg of goat in a dish and rub half the marinade over it. Save the other half for later use. Leave the leg of goat at room temperature for 3-4 hours.

Set the barbecue at medium heat and grill for an hour or until done. When it is cooked, slice and pour remaining marinade over. Serve with potato salad. ❖

Leg of Lamb with Mint

(Coscia d'agnello alla menta)

Serves 8

Ingredients

1	leg of lamb
3	ripe tomatoes
3	branches hyssop
2	branches savory
2	branches sage
1	tsp sea salt (optional)
4	garlic cloves
2	oz white wine
6	potatoes, peeled and quartered
1/4	cup oil
1/4	tsp fresh black pepper
1/2	cup mint

Method

In a roasting pan, place all the ingredients except for the potatoes. Rub all the spices into the leg, and marinate for about 2 hours.

Bake at 350° F. for 20 minutes. Then add potatoes and coat them in the lamb marinade. Bake for another 1-1/2 hours or until done.

Take out lamb and potatoes in serving dish. Strain juice. Remove excess oil, and use as a sauce over the lamb. Serve with steamed escarole or spinach. ❖

Hot Soup and Cold Dinner

(Zuppa calda, carne fredda)

Serves 8-10

Ingredients

1	lb veal shoulder
1	lb beef shoulder
5	pints cold water
4	onions, chopped
2	carrots, sliced
2	ripe tomatoes, peeled and seeded
4	bay leaves
6	juniper berries
2	garlic cloves, minced
6	leaves spinach or romaine lettuce
1	cup uncooked rice or pasta
	salt and pepper to taste

Sauce for Cold Meat

	juice of 1 lemon
2	garlic cloves, minced
1/2	cup fresh parsley, chopped
2	Tbsp olive oil
	salt and pepper to taste

Method

Cut fat from the meat. Place meat in a large pot of cold water. Soak for an hour. Drain, refill with cold water and bring to boil. Skim foam. Simmer for an hour.

Add vegetables. Simmer for another half an hour until vegetables are cooked. Remove meat and cool. Bring the same stock and vegetables to boil. Add rice or pasta and simmer for 20 minutes before serving. Serve with freshly-grated parmiggiano.

When meat is cool, slice, combine sauce ingredients. Pour sauce over. Decorate with parsley sprigs or lemon wedges before serving. ❖

Oxtail Stew with Potatoes

(Coda di manzo con patate)

Serves 6

If you use veal instead of beef oxtail, remember that veal cooks in approximately half the cooking time.

Ingredients

2	lbs oxtail
2	onions, chopped
1	stalk celery chopped
2	garlic cloves, chopped
2	bay leaves
6	juniper berries
1/4	tsp allspice
4	tomatoes, peeled and seeds removed
4	Tbsp olive oil
7	potatoes, peeled and quartered
1	cup red wine
10	sprigs parsley
	salt and pepper to taste

Method

Trim the fat from the meat. Soak in cold water for 1/2 hour. Soak potatoes in cold water until ready to use.

In a pan, add oil, drained meat, wine and all the vegetables except the tomatoes, potatoes and parsley. Cover the pan and simmer for 30 minutes, turning occasionally.

Preheat oven to 275° F. Finish cooking in the oven. Stir and add tomatoes, potatoes and parsley. If necessary, add more water. Cook for another 1 − 1-1/2 hours or until meat is fork tender.

Serve as a casserole or with a salad.

Tower Hamburgers

Serves 16

Every summer, there is a huge family gathering at my house, when I serve about 100 hamburgers to a bunch of clamouring children. My home-made hamburgers stacked high on a platter, each topped with my very own pickles, onions and tomatoes, is a sight to behold. That's why the Gallo nephews and nieces have dubbed them Tower Hamburgers.

Ingredients

4-1/2	lbs freshly ground beef
2	cups wheat germ
2	eggs, slightly beaten
1/4	cup white wine
5	sprigs parsley, minced
2	branches savory, minced
2	branches hyssop, minced
4	borage leaves, minced
4	sage leaves, minced
4	green onions, mince white part only
1/4	tsp cayenne
2	cloves garlic, minced
	salt and pepper to taste

Method

Combine all ingredients and mix well. Let stand for 10-15 minutes. Shape into 16 large hamburgers.

Grill on hot barbecue. Garnish with sliced tomatoes, red onions and sliced pickles. Serve with mustard and ketchup in Italian kaiser buns.

If you make the hamburgers ahead of time, you can wrap them in single layers in waxed paper, and freeze until required. ❖

Ham with Brandied Cherries

(Prosciutto cotto alle ciliege)

Serves 50

When I first came to Canada, I found the hams a little too salty for my taste, and this prompted me to improve on them.

After reading and researching and asking different people, I finally found a large pre-cooked ham without any brand name that was relatively inexpensive. This is the result of my efforts.

It's so popular that, over the years, I must have cooked at least 35 of these hams, and everyone invariably asks me for this recipe. I use a chicken rack with one of those roasting pans so that the ham doesn't touch the water. The steam will help to desalt the ham.

Ingredients

24	lbs ham
3	pints water
2	bay leaves
1	sprig rosemary
1	red peppercorn
1	Tbsp cloves
50	cloves for decoration
1/2	cup gin

Method

Preheat oven to 300° F.

Place all ingredients except the ham and gin into the roasting pan. Put chicken rack on top. Trim some of the fat from the ham. Make geometric incisions in the top of the ham. Insert 50 cloves in the incisions. Place ham on rack and pour gin over.

Lightly cover ham with foil. Bake, allowing 10 minutes per lb. Baste with juice from pan at least 3 times within the cooking period. Remove from the oven when done.

Glaze

3	cups brown sugar
3	Tbsp powdered mustard
4	Tbsp maple syrup
4	Tbsp flour
1/2	cup raspberry vinegar
50	brandied cherries for decorating
50	toothpicks

In a large dish, mix all glazing ingredients. Place ham in a baking dish. Pour glazing mixture over and replace in the oven. Bake at 300° F for about 3 minutes until glazing melts.

Baste ham with glaze and turn heat up to 400° F for 5 minutes until the glaze caramelizes. Remove from the oven and continue to baste until glaze is firm.

Place each of 50 cherries on a toothpick and stick them into the ham. Slice ham and serve with peaches. ❖

Old-Fashioned Gelatine of Pig

(Gelatina di maiale)

Serves 10

My mother, Maria Prezio Gallo, makes the best gelatine of pig in the world! Although she is now 86, she still makes this every year and gives a jar to each of her 8 children.

Ingredients

2	pig's feet
1	pig's tongue
2	pig's ears
1	pig's heart
1/2	lb pig skin
2	pig shanks
1	pig's lips
6	leaves sage
1	peppercorn
5	bay leaves
2	cups wine vinegar

Method

Clean meat well and let stand in a bowl of water for 2-3 hours. Place meat in a pan and cover with water. Bring to the boil. Skim off the foam. Add spices and lower heat. Cook until fork-tender.

Take meat out of water. Tie a cheesecloth across a strainer and pour the liquid through. Place the liquid back in the pan and add wine vinegar to taste. Bring to boil for 5 minutes.

Debone the meat and place it in a deep dish. Pour 1-2 cups of liquid over the meat. Cover with a dish for one hour. Then pour some more liquid over. Keep adding liquid till the meat is entirely covered.

In the old days, the meat was covered with lard, and it was only removed just before serving. ❖

Pork Chops with Juniper

(Costolette di maiale al ginepro)

Serves 6

Ingredients

6	pork chops
10-15	sprigs parsley
10	juniper berries, crushed
1	cup sparkling Rosé wine
4	leaves fresh sage
1/2	tsp cayenne
1/2	tsp ginger, ground
1/4	cup olive oil
2	Tbsp corn meal
2	onions, chopped
1	sweet or hot red pepper
4	oz (about 3) large mushrooms, sliced
2	garlic cloves, minced
2	bay leaves
	salt to taste

Method

Preheat oven to 350° F.

Trim the fat off the pork chops. Place in a dish with Juniper berries, wine, parsley, sage, cayenne, ginger and salt. Turn chops until well coated.

Heat oil in a frying pan. Fry chops for 1 minute on each side. Remove and place in a baking dish. Sprinkle with cornmeal.

In a frying pan, add onions, pepper, mushrooms and garlic. Cook for one minute. Pour over pork chops. Add bay leaves. Cover with foil and bake for 30 minutes. ❖

Pork Tenderloin

(Filetto di maiale con finocchio selvatico)

Serves 5

This is another old recipe which has weathered the years and remains a family favourite. Its advantage is that it is both quick and easy to whip up. It needs almost no preparation and takes less than half an hour to cook.

Ingredients

3	lbs pork tenderloin, cut diagonally
1/2	cup white wine
2	garlic cloves, minced
1	Tbsp fennel seeds
2	Tbsp parsley
2	oz olive oil
	salt and pepper to taste

Method

Barely cover bottom of non-stick frying pan with olive oil. Add all ingredients over high heat, shaking pan constantly. Cook till liquid evaporates and meat is a nice brown in colour.

Sprinkle parsley before serving. Serve with potatoes, steamed rice or peas. ❖

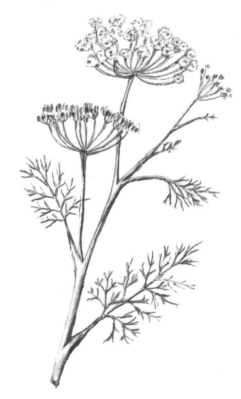

Tri-Colour Paté

(Paté tricolore)

Serves 20

Pippo, a pastry chef from Sicily who was a guest in our home, loves paté. He said that, although he has been to France and savoured many different kinds of good paté, he had never tasted one like mine!

This paté is a favourite of mine because its colours come from liver, chicken, pork and spinach. In cooking, I use a bread pan as a bain-marie for baking the paté because the paté dish fits so nicely into it.

Ingredients

1	lb pork belly	
1	lb whole chicken breasts	
1	lb chicken liver	
1/2	cup gin	
1	tsp Rita's Special Spice	
2	bunches spinach	

The day before, rinse liver, trim fat. Trim skin of pork belly and cut lengthwise.

Rinse chicken breast with cold water and trim fat. Place in a dish and add gin. Add spiced salt. Cover and refrigerate overnight.

Wash spinach and soak in salt and water. Rinse, cut and place in a pan, turning occasionally. Keep covered over low heat till cooked. Drain.

1	cup gin	
1/4	cup butter	
1	garlic clove	
4	tsp flour	
1-1/2	Tbsp butter for greasing dish and topping paté	

With the back of a chopper, pound the garlic into the pork belly, folding the garlic into the belly and vice versa. Continue for at least 3 minutes.

Place butter, pork belly and chicken breast in a frying pan. Keep turning over medium heat for 2 minutes. Add 1/2 cup gin. Cook for a minute more, turning continuously.

Take pan off burner. Remove chicken breast and cover for later use.

Remove about 3/4 of pork belly and place in a fine blender for later use.

In the same frying pan with the remaining pork belly, add liver. Cook over high heat for a minute, continuously shaking. Add remaining gin. Cook for another minute. Remove.

In the same blender with the pork belly, add spinach. Blend for a minute. Scrape the sides. Add flour. Blend for a few seconds. Remove and place in a dish.

Rinse out blender completely. Add liver and remaining pork belly. Blend until a fine velvet consistency is achieved.

Butter 12" x 4" paté dish. Line bottom and side with spinach mixture. Pat evenly. But leave enough for the top.

Cut chicken into fine slices. Line with chicken slices over spinach mixture. Leave enough again for the top.

Place all the liver mixture on top of Chicken Slices. Pat it down again. Arrange chicken slices over the liver mixture. Top with spinach mixture.

Knock the paté dish gently against the top of the counter 3 or 4 times so that the ingredients sit well.

Preheat the oven to 400° F. Place paté dish in a bread pan. Place enough water in the bread pan to surround 3/4 of the paté dish. Bake for 25 minutes. Cool. Turn it out on a serving dish.

Refrigerate for a day or two before serving.

Meat Pie Crust

This makes enough pastry for 2 small pies or a large one. You can also use vegetarian fillings such as the Eggplant Tiella.

Ingredients

4	cups all-purpose flour
1	tsp salt
1/2	cup white wine
1/4	tsp baking powder
1	cup lard
1/4	cup butter
1	tsp rosemary, juniper and caraway, freshly ground and blended
1/4	tsp cayenne
1	egg yolk for brushing
1	Tbsp red wine, also for brushing

Method

In a bowl, combine all dry ingredients. Cut in butter and lard. With a fork, gradually stir wine into flour mixture until it is absorbed.

Make a ball. Wrap in waxed paper and chill until ready for use.

Veal and Pork Filling

2	lbs veal shoulder
1	lb pork shoulder
2	oz red wine
1	oz olive oil
2	garlic cloves, minced
1	tsp fine spice
1	leek, chopped
2	parsnips, sliced
2	Tbsp cornmeal
2	Tbsp parsley, minced
	salt and pepper to taste

Method

Cut veal and pork shoulder into chunks. Add wine, garlic and fine spice. Mix well. Marinate for at least 1 hour.

In a frying pan, sauté meat with leek and parsnips for 2-3 minutes. Add cornmeal, parsley, salt and pepper.

Remove from burner and cool.

Roll out pastry, dividing it so there is enough for the top. Line 12" x 10" x 2 1/2" dish. Add meat filling. Cover with remaining pastry.

Seal edges and crimp with fork. Make vents in top of crust with fork in a decorative manner. Brush with egg yolk mixed with wine.

Bake in preheated oven at 400° F for 5 minutes. Reduce heat to 350° F and bake for 45 minutes.

When done, remove and cool slightly before serving. ❖

Rita's Special Spice

This is a variation of a spice which my grandmother used to make. She had to tie a handkerchief round her face because the pounding made her sneeze.

Ingredients

6	Tbsp coarse salt
1	stick cinnamon (1")
4	cloves
4	dry hot peppers
1	Tbsp peppercorns
4	cardamoms
1	Tbsp sage
1/2	tsp thyme
1/2	tsp caraway
1	tsp savory
1/2	tsp tarragon
1/2	tsp cumin
2	bay leaves

Method

If you are using a blender, make sure you keep turning it on and off so you do not destroy the essential oils.

Store in glass jars. Keep tightly sealed.

This is a good spice for beef or pork, and excellent for fish. Use 1/2 tsp for every 4-5 lbs. ❖

BREADS

Cornbread
Maple Almond Bread
White Bread and Hidden Pizza
Multi-Grain Bread
Mastazzole
Frese
Aniseed Bread
Sweet Pumpkin Bread

Cornbread

(Pane di granoturco)

Makes 4 loaves

Ingredients

2	envelopes of dry active yeast
2	cups water
2	Tbsp sugar
2	cups cornmeal
2	cups cornflour
4	cups all-purpose flour
2	oz olive oil
1	egg, slightly beaten
2	Tbsp salt
2	cups water

Method

Dissolve sugar in warm water. Sprinkle yeast on top. Let stand for 10 minutes. Mix all the flour together, save 1/4 cup of the all-purpose to flour board.

In a bowl, add olive oil, egg, salt, and water. Turn flour on rolling board. Make a well in the centre of the flour. Stir in the yeast mixture. Mix well. With a rotating motion of the hand, work in the rest of the liquids. Continue until all flour is absorbed.

Turn dough out onto lightly floured surface. Knead for 5-8 minutes. Shape into a smooth ball and place in a buttered bowl. Cover with a towel. Leave in a warm place for 1 hour or until dough doubles in size.

Punch down the dough and turn onto a lightly floured surface. Divide into 4 portions. Shape into round loaves. Place on a greased and floured cookie sheet. Cover for 1 hour and let rise. With a knife, make a checkerboard design on top of bread.

Bake at 375° F for 5 minutes. Reduce heat to 350° F. Continue baking for about 1 hour or until done. Loaves should be golden and sound hollow when tapped. ❖

Maple Almond Bread

Makes 3 loaves

Ingredients

2	envelopes of dry active yeast
2	cups water
1	Tbsp sugar
1 1/2	cups warm milk
2	Tbsp butter
5	cups whole wheat flour
5	cups rye flour
2 1/2	cups all-purpose flour
1/2	cup blanched almonds, finely chopped
2	Tbsp maple syrup
1	Tbsp salt

Method

Preheat oven to 375° F.

Dissolve the sugar in warm water. Sprinkle yeast on top. Let stand for 10 minutes. Melt butter in warm milk.

Mix flour and almonds, making a well in the centre. Stir in the yeast mixture. Mix well. Add milk mixture, syrup and salt. Work in last of flour with a rotating motion of the hand. Continue until all flour is blended.

Turn dough out onto lightly floured surface. Knead for 5-8 minutes. Shape into a smooth ball and place in a buttered bowl. Cover with a damp cloth. Leave in a warm place for 1 hour or until dough doubles in size.

Punch down the dough and turn onto a lightly floured surface. Divide into 3 portions. Form into loaves. Place on a greased and floured cookie sheet. Cover for 1 hour and let rise.

Bake at 375° F for 5 minutes. Reduce heat to 350° F. Continue baking for about 1 hour or until done. Loaves should be golden and sound hollow when tapped.

This bread will keep for 2-3 months if well-wrapped and frozen. ❖

Photograph by Liana Tumino

Cornbread
Recipe page 102

Photograph by Liana Tumino

Tri-Colour Paté
Recipe page 99

Floral Borage Dip   *Anchovies with Capers*
Recipe page 139   Recipe page 149

Photograph by Liana Tumino

Multigrain Bread
Recipe page 108

Cornbread
Recipe page 102

Photograph by Liana Tumino

Tri-Colour Paté
Recipe page 99

Floral Borage Dip   *Anchovies with Capers*
Recipe page 139   Recipe page 149

White Bread and Hidden Pizza

(Pane bianco e pizza imbrogliata)

Makes: 3 loaves of bread
1 large pizza

Ingredients for Sourdough

2	cups lukewarm water
2	cups all-purpose flour
2	Tbsp yeast
2	Tbsp sugar

Method

Sourdough must be prepared 24 hours prior to baking in order to allow it to sour and rise. (It should triple in size.)

Place water, sugar and yeast in a deep dish. Cover for 10 minutes. Stir-in flour briskly with a fork until absorbed. Cover and let stand for 24 hours.

Ingredients for Bread and Pizza Dough

16	cups flour
3	cups potatoes (approximately 6 or 7 small potatoes), boiled and mashed
4	cups hot water
3	Tbsp salt
3	Tbsp olive oil

Method

Prepare water, salt and oil together. Pile 15 cups of flour on a rolling board. Make a well. Place potatoes and sourdough in the middle. Use a squeezing motion with one hand to work-in potatoes, sourdough and flour. At the same time, slowly pour in water. With other hand, switch to a rotating motion until last of water and flour is worked in. Lightly flour surface of board and with both hands, turn dough out and knead until smooth. This should take 5 to 8 minutes. Shape into a ball and place in a buttered bowl. Cover and let stand for 1 to 1-1/2 hours or until doubled.

Take half of dough (save other half for pizza) and punch it down. Divide into 3 parts, and shape into loaves. Place on cookie sheet which has been covered with parchment paper. Bake in preheated 350° F oven for 45 minutes or until golden.

Ingredients for Pizza Filling

15	slices prosciutto
2	cups mozzarella cheese
1	cup grated zucchini
4	eggs, slightly beaten
4	Tbsp parsley, minced
3	Tbsp olive oil
1	2" x 11" x 15" pan

Method

Use 1 Tbsp oil to lightly oil pan. Place dough on floured board. Lightly sprinkle more flour over the dough and roll it to at least twice the size of the pan and 1/2 inch thick. Place dough over pan. Half the dough should fall over one side in order to later function as a lid and seal the pizza. Spread 1 Tbsp oil on dough sitting in pan. Place all ingredients (except last bit of oil) evenly inside. Gently pull sides over filling and close lid. Pinch dough together to seal the pizza. Spread olive oil over top. Pizza should rest 20 minutes before baking. Place in preheated 400° F oven for 10 minutes and lower oven to 350° F for 40 minutes or until golden. ❖

Multi-Grain Bread

Makes 6 loaves

I can remember vividly as a child the times my mother and grandmother used to make bread. They made about 200 lbs at a time, some of which was dried in the oven and stored for later use. All the neighbourhood children would come to watch. Each one always got a piece, the little ones with olive oil and sugar sprinkled on top, while the older ones got olive oil and hot pepper.

Most people don't realize just how easy it is to bake bread, and what great therapy kneading the dough is! I've made some changes to my mother's recipe by adding molasses and wheat germ, and by substituting sourdough for a starter, but it still tastes the same old-fashioned way.

Ingredients

Yeast Mixture

3	envelopes yeast
3	Tbsp brown sugar
3	cups lukewarm water
4	cups all-purpose flour

In a small bowl, dissolve brown sugar in water. Sprinkle yeast over top. Cover and let stand for 10 minutes. Stir briskly with a fork.

Add the flour a cupful at a time. Blend well with a wooden spoon. Let stand for 1 hour, covered with a damp cloth in a warm place away from draughts, or until dough doubles in size.

Milk Mixture

1	cup warm milk
1/2	cup butter
2	Tbsp honey
2	Tbsp molasses
2	eggs, slightly beaten

Melt butter in warm milk. Combine all ingredients and set aside for later use.

Flour mixture

6	cups all-purpose flour
2	cups oat bran
8	cups whole wheat flour
8	cups dark rye flour
2	cups wheat germ
4	cups water
3	Tbsp salt

On a clean board or counter, combine all the dry ingredients except 1 cup of all-purpose flour. Make a well in the centre. Add yeast and milk mixtures. Stir well. Add water a cupful at a time, stirring with rotating motion until water is absorbed.

Make a large ball. Knead and rotate until smooth, adding the reserved flour if necessary. Continue kneading for 8-10 minutes until the dough is smooth. Place in a large buttered bowl. Cover with a towel and keep in a warm place away from draughts for 1-1 1/2 hours, or until dough doubles in size.

Punch down the dough. Divide into 6 and shape into loaves. Punch dough flat again and sprinkle with filling. Roll dough into shape and tuck sides underneath. Place on two cookie sheets sprinkled with cornmeal. Cover with a tea towel and let rise until double in size.

Preheat the oven to 375° F. Bake the loaves for 10 minutes. Lower heat to 350° F and continue baking for 35 minutes or until done. Loaves should be crisp on the outside and sound hollow when tapped. Cool on wire racks.

If you are freezing the bread, remove from the oven 10 minutes before it is ready. Do not wrap bread for freezing for at least 3-4 hours. Wrap with waxed paper. Rewrap in foil. Place in plastic bag and freeze.

When ready to eat, bake at 250° F for 10 minutes.

Herbal Filling

1/2	cup parsley, minced
1/2	tsp savory
1/2	tsp hyssop
1/2	tsp hot pepper
1/2	tsp cayenne

Mix all ingredients together. Stuff dough.

Vegetable Filling

2	cups borage or spinach, chopped
1	cup gruyere cheese, grated
1	cup fontina cheese, grated
2	Tbsp savory, chopped
1	Tbsp hyssop
1/4	tsp nutmeg, freshly ground
1/4	tsp hot pepper

| 1/4 | tsp black pepper, freshly ground |

Mix all ingredients together. Stuff dough.

Meat and Cheese Filling

1	lb hot or sweet sausage
1/2	cup swiss cheese
2	cups pecorino cheese
1/2	tsp tarragon
1/2	tsp savory
1/2	tsp hyssop
1/4	tsp black pepper, freshly ground
3	tsp semolina
1	Tbsp butter

Method

These recipes are enough for 3 loaves and should be eaten fresh.

Place cut sausage and butter in a frying pan. Sauté over medium heat for a few minutes. Cool. Mix all ingredients together. Stuff dough. ❖

Mastazzole

This bread is traditionally given to teething babies and was originally baked without the walnuts.

Ingredients

2	lbs honey
8	cups all-purpose flour
4	eggs
2	Tbsp baking powder
1/2	tsp cinnamon
2	Tbsp orange peel
1	cup walnuts, chopped (optional)
1	egg yolk for brushing
1	Tbsp cold water for brushing

Method

Preheat oven to 325° F.

Beat egg and honey for 2 minutes on a rolling board. Mix the dry ingredients. Make a well in the centre. Add egg

mixture with a rotating motion quickly, until flour is absorbed.

Roll out a piece of dough 8" x 4" long. Place on a cookie sheet over parchment paper. Roll out a smaller piece about the length and width of a cord, and decorate it in a zigzag fashion on top of a larger piece. Brush with egg yolk and cold water.

Bake at 325° F for 30-40 minutes until golden. Cool before slicing and serving.

These are excellent for any snack and they freeze well. ❖

Frese

Serves 5

In the north of Italy, they serve "bruschetta", but in the south, we serve "frese". It is made with the same dough as the multi-grain bread. My grandmother used to make really huge frese, but now I make them the same size as bagels. They are good for travelling. We take them along whenever we go to Florida.

They are cut in two with a fork and dried in the oven so that they will keep indefinitely. We usually serve them with a tomato salad dressing or with a vinegar, oil and garlic sauce.

Fresh Tomato Salad Ingredients

2	tomatoes, diced
1	tsp oregano
1	clove garlic, halved
1/4	cup olive oil
1	tsp capers, rinsed and chopped

Mix all ingredients in a dish and spoon generously over the top.

Vinegar, Oil and Garlic Dressing

2	garlic cloves
2	oz olive oil
1	oz raspberry vinegar
1	Tbsp oregano
1/2	tsp hot pepper

Rub garlic over 5 frese. In a bowl, mix all other ingredients. Pour over frese and serve. ❖

Aniseed Bread

(Taralli con anice)

Makes 50 rolls

This is a very old recipe for aniseed bread which we used to have for breakfast. They are shaped like bagels. My mother still cuts them in two and dries them in the oven. They are dunked in hot milk as cereal.

Ingredients

2	Tbsp yeast
2	Tbsp sugar
2	cups warm water
2	cups all-purpose flour

Method

Dissolve the sugar and yeast in warm water. Let stand covered for 10 minutes.

Add flour to make a starter. Cover with a damp cloth and let rise for an hour or until it doubles in size.

4	cups warm milk
1/2	cup butter
1/2	cup sugar
1	Tbsp salt
1	Tbsp aniseed

In a bowl, beat sugar, salt, eggs and aniseed together. Add milk and set aside for later use.

15	cups all-purpose flour
1	lb rye

Turn flour and rye out on rolling board and mix together. Make a well in the centre. With a rotating motion, add the starter. Then add the egg mixture. Continue until flour is absorbed.

Shape dough into a ball. Knead for 5-8 minutes until smooth. The dough should be firm. Cover with a linen cloth until it doubles in size.

Roll dough into 6" strips on unfloured surface. Form into a circle. Line 4 cookie sheets with parchment paper. Place taralli 2" apart.

Cover the first tray with a linen cloth. This will facilitate baking. Continue until all the dough has been used. Let stand for at least 1/2 hour or until dough springs back to the touch.

8	pints water
4	Tbsp honey

Bring water and honey to boil. Drop taralli in. After wetting, remove with slotted spoon. Replace in same trays and bake at 450° F for 10 minutes. Reduce heat to 350° F and bake for 15 minutes or until golden.

Serve with marmalade or honey.

Sweet Pumpkin Bread

(Pane dolce di zucca)

Makes 2 loaves

Ingredients

4-1/4	cups all-purpose flour
2	cups of pumpkin filling or steamed pumpkin
1/4	cup shortening
2	eggs
1	cup apples, diced (1 medium apple)
1/2	cup raisins, rinsed in hot water
1/2	cup brown sugar
1/2	cup sour cream
1/4	tsp salt
1	Tbsp baking powder
1/2	tsp baking soda
1/4	tsp cinnamon
1/4	tsp nutmeg

Method

In a bowl, sift together dry ingredients; flour, salt, nutmeg, baking powder, baking soda and cinnamon. In a blender, place eggs, sugar, shortening, apples, raisins and pumpkin and blend for 2 minutes. Then add sour cream and stir. Place liquid mixture with dry ingredients until flour is absorbed and becomes lumpy.

Preheat oven at 400° F. Place ingredients in 2 - 10" x 4" x 3" oiled pans. Bake for 10 minutes. Reduce heat to 350° F and bake for 30 minutes or until golden. ❖

DESSERTS

Many of my desserts are made with fresh fruit or my own preserves, thus rendering them very healthy. I also use quite a lot of herbal syrups. I like to maintain that delicate balance between health and enjoyment.

I never serve desserts immediately after dinner. This allows the food to be properly digested. This way, my guests enjoy everything I serve them.

Grandparents' Favourite Dessert
Herbal Tea
Apples Stuffed with Amaretti
Borage Tea
Peaches in White Vermouth
Pear and Nectarine Delight
My Favourite Dark Fruit Cake
Strawberry and Pineapple
Strawberries with Oranges and Lemon
Anna's Amaretti
Lemon Verbena Cheesecake
Butternut Torte
Rosa's Orange Sponge Cake
Red Currant Topping
Kiwi Topping
Peach and Berry Dessert in Angelica Syrup
Blueberry Pie
Giuliana & Melissa's Coconut Honey Almond Chocolate Chip Cookies
Marco, Maria & Melissa's Wheatgerm Maple Syrup Muffins
Sisa's Almond Cookies
Mascarpone Cups
Chocolate Chestnuts
Walnut Oil Crust

Grandparents' Favourite Dessert

(Favorito dei Nonni)

Serves 8

This is my parents' favourite dessert. It's delicious served hot with vanilla ice cream at about 4 o'clock in the afternoon. We usually finish with a herbal tea.

Ingredients

7	cooking apples
2	Tbsp butter
2	oz Vermouth
1/2	cup maple syrup
3	Tbsp brown sugar
3	Tbsp desiccated coconut
1	cup almonds, ground
1	cup graham crumbs
1/4	tsp cinnamon
1/4	tsp cloves
	juice of 1 lemon

Method

Preheat oven to 300° F. Butter a baking dish. Mix all ingredients well. Pat into baking dish. Bake for about 1/2 hour or until apples are tender.

Serve with vanilla ice cream.

Herbal Tea

Serves 8

This is my grandmother's recipe and is very easy to prepare.

Ingredients

2-1/2	pints water
3	bay leaves
1	Tbsp spearmint
2	Tbsp mallow
1/2	tsp aniseed
1	stick licorice, about 1"

Method

Place all ingredients in a covered saucepan. Bring to boil. Turn off heat and let rest for 10-15 minutes. Serve with honey or brown sugar. ❖

Apples stuffed with amaretti

(Mele ripieni all'amaretti)

Serves 6

This dessert works best with amaretti biscuits, which are packaged and available at any Italian store. Remember that your apples should be at room temperature.

Ingredients

6	big apples, washed and cored
6	orange slices
12	little amaretti biscuits
1/2	cup amaretto liqueur
1/2	cup golden raisins
2	Tbsp butter
2	Tbsp sugar

Method

Preheat the oven to 350° F.

Plump raisins with hot water and squeeze liquid out. Soak raisins in amaretto.

Butter a casserole dish. Sprinkle sugar on the bottom. Arrange orange slices over it.

Mix amaretti biscuits with raisins and stuff into apples. Place apples on top of orange slices. Cover with foil and bake for 30 minutes.

Serve apples upside down with orange slice on top.

Borage Tea
(Tè alla borraggine)

Serves 4-6

Ingredients

20	leaves orange mint
10	leaves bergamot
30	borage flowers
20	mallow flowers
4	cups water

Method

Bring water to boil. Add all other ingredients. Turn heat off. Cover and let stand for 10-15 minutes before serving. ❖

Peaches in White Vermouth
(Pesche con vermouth bianco)

Serves 10

Peaches are a great favourite in our home, and we buy them by the bushel. I make at least 50 jars of preserves of Golden Jubilee peaches. This recipe from Italy has been adapted for our use.

Peaches make a very tasty dessert, and can be served either with white vermouth or red wine. It's ideal for very informal occasions. Members of the family can peel and slice their own peach and drop it into their own wine glass.

Ingredients

10	large Golden Jubilee peaches, peeled and quartered
2	cups white vermouth
1	lemon rind, grated
10	slices lemon
10	pineapple sage leaves

Method

Place quartered peaches in a bowl. Pour white vermouth and add grated lemon. Chill.

Spoon peaches and vermouth into glasses. Decorate with lemon slices and pineapple sage leaves.

Hint: To prevent slices of peaches from turning brown, squeeze some lemon juice over them. ❖

Pear and Nectarine Delight
(Delizia di pere e noce pesco)

Serves 10

Ingredients
Crust

2	cups bread crumbs
2	eggs, slightly beaten
1/2	cup white wine
3	Tbsp sugar
1/4	cup butter, melted
1/4	tsp nutmeg, freshly ground

Topping

7	large pears, peeled and sliced (1/4 inch)
2	nectarines, peeled and sliced (1/4 inch)
1	juice of lemon
2	juice of tangerines
1	peel of tangerine, grated
2	Tbsp sugar
2	Tbsp Cointreau
1	Tbsp cornstarch

Method

Place bread crumbs, butter, sugar and eggs in a dish and mix well. Butter 13-1/2 inch flan or baking dish and press mixture evenly onto the bottom and sides of dish.

In a large mixing bowl, place all other ingredients and toss gently. Place pears and nectarines on top of crust and arrange decoratively. Pour juice over top. Cover with aluminum foil and bake at 350°F for 30-35 minutes. ❖

My Favourite Dark Fruit Cake

(Torta di frutta candita)

Makes 3 loaves

This cake is dedicated to all my English clients whose traditional fruit cakes inspired me to create this one. I have been making this cake for the past 27 years and it is the perfect gift for all my friends at Christmas.

Ingredients

2	lbs sultana raisins
1	lb currants
1-1/2	lbs golden raisins
2	cups brandy

2-3 days ahead, prepare the dried fruit by soaking in hot water for 1 hour. Rinse with cold water and drain. Bake on a cookie sheet in oven at 150° F for 3 hours. Remove from oven. Pour brandy over and leave covered for 2-3 days in the refrigerator.

Line 3 loaf pans 10" x 4" x 2-1/2" with heavy brown or parchment paper, and butter thoroughly.

1/4	lb candied pineapples
1/2	lb candied cherries
3/4	lb dates
1/2	lb figs
1/2	lb candied citron
1/4	lb candied orange and lemon peel
1	cup blanched almond halves
1	cup filberts, coarsely chopped
1/2	cup pecans, coarsely chopped

Chop all dried and candied fruit. Combine with nuts and set aside.

1	lb unsalted butter
2	cups brown sugar
12	eggs
2	tsp vanilla
3-1/2	cups all-purpose flour
1/2	tsp salt
2	tsp cinnamon
2	tsp nutmeg
1/2	tsp allspice
1/2	tsp ginger
1/2	tsp cloves

Cream butter and brown sugar thoroughly. Add eggs one at a time, then vanilla, and continue to beat for 3-4 minutes.

Sift together all the dry ingredients. Add half the flour mixture to the butter. Add the other half of the flour mixture to the fruit and nut mixture, mixing well. Add the dry mixture to the wet mixture in 3 portions, mixing well after each addition. Fold in the brandied fruit. Turn into the prepared pans.

Bake at 275° F for 2-1/2 - 3 hours or until done when tested with a toothpick. Remove from pan and set on a rack to cool, with paper still attached. Pour 1/2 cup brandy over the cake.

When cooled, wrap cake tightly in waxed paper, then aluminum foil. Store in a cool place and pour another 1/2 cup brandy over the cake every 2-3 months. It will keep up to a year. Remove the heavy paper only when ready to serve. ❖

Strawberry and Pineapple

(Fragole e ananas fresche)

Serves 6

Ingredients

1	pineapple, peeled and diced
1/2	tsp baking soda
1	pint strawberries
1/4	cup lime liqueur or Cointreau
5	lemon verbena leaves, minced
6	lemon verbena leaves for garnish
	juice of 1 lemon
	juice of 2 oranges
4	Tbsp sugar

Method

Sprinkle baking soda on pineapple.

Mix all remaining ingredients except sugar and the whole verbena leaves.

Sprinkle the sugar on top and refrigerate. Just before serving, toss to mix the sugar. Serve in sherbet glasses and garnish with whole verbena leaves. ❖

Butternut Torte
Recipe page 120

My Favourite Dark Fruit Cake
Recipe page 114

A Little More Than Date Squares
Recipe page 155

DESSERTS **115**

Blueberry Pie
Recipe page 122

Scauille
Recipe page 40

Italian Turnovers
Recipe page 41

Turdilli
Recipe page 41

Rosa's Orange Sponge Cake
Recipe page 121

Cecilia's Chocolate Cheesecake
Recipe page 163

Giuliana and Melissa's Coconut Honey Almond Chocolate Chip Cookies
Recipe page 123

Anna's Amaretti *Mastazolle*
Recipe page 119 *Recipe page 109*

Photograph by Liana Tumino

Strawberries with Oranges and Lemon

(Fragole all' arancia e limone)

Serves 6

I love this dessert because it's so refreshing and the different colours please my eye. I particularly enjoy its clean taste, but my husband Federico likes to drown his in Cointreau or Cognac.

Ingredients

2	quarts strawberries
2	Tbsp salt
2	lemons
2	oranges
1	Tbsp baking soda
3	Tbsp brown sugar

Method

Wet oranges and lemons. Rub baking soda on skins and rinse again. Place strawberries in cold water with 2 Tbsp salt. Leave for a minute then rinse again with cold water.

Cut tops off strawberries and quarter. Place in a glass bowl. Grate 1 orange and 1 lemon coarsely over top of strawberries. Pour juice of 2 lemons and juice of 2 oranges over top.

Sprinkle brown sugar over and refrigerate. Just before serving, mix well. Serve on its own or with ice cream if desired. ❖

Anna's Amaretti

(Amaretti all'Anna)

Makes 6 dozen

This recipe is another closely-guarded secret from my husband's family. It's a great hit at parties and family gatherings, and I finally persuaded Federico's cousin, Anna, to part with this rare gem. The crunchy cookies freeze well and retain their distinctive flavour even after 2 or 3 months.

Ingredients

4	eggs
7	cups almonds, finely ground
12	sour almonds, finely ground
2	cups vanilla sugar
1/4	cup amaretto liqueur
3	Tbsp flour (to dip your hands in)

Method

Beat the eggs with the sugar for 2-3 minutes. Add almonds and sour almonds. Blend until liquid is absorbed. Then dip your hands in flour. Take a piece of the dough about the size of a walnut and roll into a ball.

Ingredients

2	Tbsp sugar to dip the amaretti in
10	candied cherries, cut in half
28	whole almonds
24	whole coffee beans

Method

Dip each amaretto ball in sugar. Then press 1 cherry, almond or coffee bean on the top of each amaretto ball.

Place on a greased cookie sheet one inch apart. Bake at 350° F for 5 minutes. Turn down the heat to 300° F and bake for approx. 8-10 minutes or until lightly browned.

Wrap in waxed paper and store in plastic bag before freezing. ❖

Lemon Verbena Cheesecake

Serves 16

Ingredients

Crust

2	cups graham cracker crumbs
2	Tbsp brown sugar
1/3	cup ground almonds
3	Tbsp lemon liqueur
1/2	cup unsalted butter, melted

Filling

5	eggs, separated
1	cup sugar
1/4	tsp salt
3	Tbsp flour
1	lb cream cheese
1	cup whipping cream
2	Tbsp lemon rind, grated
2	Tbsp lemon juice
2	Tbsp lemon liqueur
7	lemon verbena leaves, minced
3	Tbsp semi-sweet chocolate, grated

Method

Combine all crust ingredients thoroughly. Press into bottom and sides of a 10" spring form pan.

Preheat oven to 300° F. Beat egg whites, half of the sugar and salt until stiff peaks form. Set aside.

Beat egg yolks, other half of sugar and flour for about 5 minutes until lemon-coloured. Add cream cheese and beat for 3 minutes.

Add whipping cream, beating another 3 seconds. Add lemon rind, juice, lemon liqueur and lemon verbena leaves. Blend well.

Fold egg whites and grated chocolate gently into egg yolk mixture. Pour into crust and bake for an hour.

Turn oven off, open oven door and let cake cool gradually for another hour.

Serve with whipping cream or desired topping. ❖

Butternut Torte

(Torta di zucca)

Ingredients

1	lb butternut squash
1	cup milk
2	envelopes unflavoured gelatine
1-1/2	cups brown sugar, firmly packed
4	eggs, separated
1	tsp cinnamon
1/4	tsp cardamom, ground
1	tsp salt
1/2	cup granulated sugar
1/2	cup sour cream
1	tsp lemon rind

Method

Preheat oven to 350° F. Bake squash in oven for an hour. Let cool slightly. Peel and scoop out seeds. Purée pulp in blender. This makes about 3 cupfuls.

In a medium saucepan, heat milk until warm. Stir in gelatine until completely dissolved. Add puréed squash, brown sugar, egg yolks, cardamom, cinnamon and salt. Stir constantly over medium heat until boiling. Let cool.

Refrigerate for about 20 minutes until slightly thickened and mixture mounds slightly when turned with a spoon.

Beat egg whites until soft peaks form. Gradually add granulated sugar and continue beating until stiff. Gently fold in the squash mixture, sour cream and lemon rind.

Pour into a 9" x 13" prepared crust, and chill at least 4 hours or overnight.

Serve with whipping cream or desired topping. ❖

Rosa's Orange Sponge Cake

This is a basic cake recipe which can be used to complement different desserts and topped with fruit, liqueur or ice cream.

You can make either an orange or a lemon sponge cake with this versatile recipe. For the lemon sponge cake, just substitute the juice and rind of a large lemon for that of the orange and lemon liqueur instead of orange liqueur.

Ingredients

3/4	cups vegetable oil
2	cups sugar
6	eggs
2	tsp orange liqueur or Grand Marnier
1	orange (grated rind and juice)
3/4	cup milk
3	cups all-purpose flour
5	tsp baking powder
1/4	tsp cardamom, ground
	pinch of salt

Method

Preheat oven to 350° F. Grease and flour a 10" tube pan.

Beat sugar and oil. Add eggs one at a time, beating well each time. Add liqueur, rind, juice and milk.

Mix flour, salt, baking powder and cardamom. Add to egg mixture and mix until all the flour is combined. The batter should be slightly thicker than cake batter.

Bake for an hour. Remove from pan and cool.

Red Currant Topping

(Gelatina di mirtilli rossi)

Serves 6

Ingredients

1	quart red currants
1/2	cup sugar
1	envelope unflavoured gelatine
1/2	cup fruit liqueur
1	oz water

Method

Wash red currants and drain in a colander.

In a wide non-stick frying pan, add red currants, sugar and liqueur. Stir for 1-2 minutes. Pour through sieve and reserve juice for later use.

Deseed red currants and replace in pan. Dissolve gelatine in water and add to juice. Add to pan and cook for 1 minute.

Cool and pour over top of cheesecake.

Kiwi Topping

Ingredients

3	kiwis, peeled, sliced in rounds
1/4	cup Cointreau
1	envelope unflavoured gelatine
1/2	cup water
1	tsp orange jelly powder

Method

Mix kiwis and Cointreau in a saucepan. Remove. Sprinkle gelatine over water. Let stand for 1 minute. Pour into saucepan and cook over medium heat, stirring constantly until gelatine dissolves completely. Add jelly powder and continue stirring until completely dissolved. Cool.

Chill in refrigerator for about 15 minutes until gelatine mixture thickens slightly. Place kiwis on top of cake. Spoon gelatine mixture slowly over kiwis. Refrigerate for at least 1 hour until fully set. ❖

Peach and Berry Dessert in Angelica Syrup

(Pesche e Mirtilli con l'angelica)

Serves 12

The colours of this desert are very beautiful.

You can make the syrup for this dessert ahead of time as it refrigerates well and can be used a month or a day later.

Ingredients

6	cups water
1	cup sugar
1	branch angelica, cut into 1" lengths
10	leaves fresh lemon verbena
3	leaves fresh lemon eucalyptus
4	leaves fresh pineapple sage leaves
2	branches myrtle
1/4	tsp cardamom, crushed
1/2	cup Triple Sec or Cointreau
10	large peaches, peeled and sliced
1	quart blueberries
1/2	quart thimble berries
2	quarts strawberries
	juice and slices of 1 lemon

Method

Combine water, sugar and all herbs in a large saucepan. Bring to boil. Simmer for 2-3 minutes. Remove from heat. Cool. Strain all leaves and branches except angelica.

Add Triple Sec, lemon juice and lemon slices. Add all the fruit to the syrup and chill before serving. ❖

Blueberry Pie

(Crostata di mirtilli)

Almond Crust Ingredients

2-1/2	cups almonds, finely ground
6	Tbsp brown sugar
2	Tbsp flour
2	Tbsp Amaretto
4	Tbsp butter
1/4	tsp nutmeg

Method

Combine ingredients well and press into a pie dish. Refrigerate until ready for use.

Filling

1	quart blueberries
1/2	cup brown sugar
2	Tbsp orange liqueur
1/4	tsp nutmeg
1/4	tsp cardamom
2	Tbsp cornstarch
2	Tbsp crushed almonds
	rind of 1 orange

Method

Rinse and drain blueberries well. Place them in a dish. Mix all other ingredients well. Fill pie crust and bake at 400° F for 5 minutes.

Reduce heat to 350° F and bake for 30-35 minutes. ❖

Giuliana & Melissa's Coconut Honey Almond Chocolate Chip Cookies

Makes about 4 dozen

My nieces Giuliana and Melissa came to visit me one weekend when they were 12 and 11 respectively. We came up with this wonderful cookie recipe and shared it with the family, who simply loved it.

Ingredients

1	cup brown sugar
1	cup butter
2	eggs
1/2	cup honey
2	tsp vanilla
2-1/2	cups all-purpose flour
1/2	tsp baking soda
1	tsp salt
1	cup chocolate chips
1	cup almonds, coarsely chopped
1	cup unsweetened desiccated coconut

Method

Preheat oven to 350° F. Lightly grease two baking sheets 11" x 15".

Cream sugar and butter until light and fluffy. Add eggs, one at a time, and beat until well combined. Add honey and vanilla.

Stir dry ingredients together. Add to the butter mixture. Mix well. Fold in chocolate chips, almonds and coconut.

Drop batter by the teaspoonful about 2" apart on cookie sheet. Bake for 8-10 minutes until golden brown. ❖

Marco, Maria & Melissa's Wheatgerm Maple Syrup Muffins

Makes 18 medium muffins

This is a recipe which my nephew and two nieces devised while on a visit to my house. They decided to combine wheatgerm and maple syrup to make these muffins. They are very nutritious and not too sweet.

Ingredients

1/4	cup butter, melted
2	eggs, beaten
1-3/4	cups milk
1/4	cup pure maple syrup
1	lemon rind, grated
2-1/2	cups all-purpose flour
2	tsp baking powder
1	cup corn meal
1/2	cup wheat germ
1/4	cup brown sugar
1	tsp salt
1/8	tsp cardamom, ground
1/4	cup raisins

Method

Wash raisins and pour boiling water over to plump them. Drain.

Preheat oven to 400°F. Grease muffin tins or line paper cups. Beat the butter and the sugar for 2 minutes at high speed. Continue beating as you add eggs and maple syrup. Then add milk and lemon rind.

Sift flour and baking powder. Stir in remaining dry ingredients and raisins. Combine wet and dry ingredients, mixing lightly until all the flour is moistened.

Fill muffin tins about 3/4 full. Sprinkle tops with sugar. Bake for 20 minutes or until brown. ❖

Sisa's Almond Cookies

(Sisa dolcini di mandorle)

Makes approximately 24 cookies

Ingredients

1-1/2	lbs roasted, lightly ground almonds
2-1/4	cups all purpose flour
1	cup vegetable oil
3	eggs, lightly beaten
1	tsp almond extract
2-1/2	tsp baking powder
1/4	tsp salt
1	cup sugar

Method

Stir together flour, almonds, baking powder and salt. Beat the eggs with the sugar and add oil and almond extract. Add dry ingredients to liquid ingredients until all flour is absorbed. Preheat oven to 350° F. Flour a rolling board. Take a piece and roll it like a log about 12 inches long. Slightly flatten it and slice 1/2" pieces. Place pieces on oiled or buttered cookie sheet. Bake in the pre-heated oven for 10-12 minutes or until slightly golden. ❖

Mascarpone Cups

(Coppe di mascarpone)

Serves 6

Ingredients

1	lb of mascarpone cheese
6	egg yolks
6	egg whites
6	Tbsp of sugar
3	Tbsp of Granatin syrup

Method

Beat the egg yolks with the sugar until they become thick and yellow in colour. Add the mascarpone cheese to the egg yolks and blend together with a spatula. Then add the Granatin while continuing to blend. Beat the egg whites until they form a peak. Gently fold the egg whites into the egg yolk mixture. Spoon into dessert cups and place in the refrigerator until served. ❖

Chocolate Chestnuts

(Castagne al cioccolato)

Makes approximately 60

Ingredients

1-1/2	lbs of dried chestnuts (available in Italian grocery stores)
1/2	cup cocoa
1	cup sugar
1	Tbsp butter
1/2	cup Crème de Café liqueur
6	cups water
1	Tbsp icing sugar

Method

Soak chestnuts for 10 minutes in water. Remove any brown skin. Rinse and place in a pot filled with 6 cups of water. Cover and bring to boil. Simmer for 20 minutes or until soft. Drain and cool. Place chestnuts in a blender along with all other ingredients. Blend until a dough-like consistency is reached. Shape into chestnut form. Refrigerate and sift icing sugar on top just before serving. ❖

Walnut Oil Crust

(Crosta di noce)

This crust tastes delicious with cheesecake filling or butternut torte.

Ingredients

2	cups walnuts, finely ground
6	Tbsp brown sugar
1	Tbsp flour
2	Tbsp Cointreau
4	Tbsp butter
1	Tbsp walnut oil, optional

Method

Preheat oven to 400° F.

Combine ingredients well. Press crumb mixture evenly over bottom and sides of 9" x 13" pan.

Bake for 6-8 minutes. Cool before adding gelatine filling. ❖

Traditional Christmas Eve Dinner Menu

(Cenone di Natale)

Serves 50

The Christmas Eve dinner was a tradition that my mother observed every year. Now that she is in her eighties, her children have begun to take turns preparing for it.

For me, this festive occasion assumed a special significance with the gathering of four generations of the Gallo family under one roof. It took me four days diligently working to reproduce the entire menu, with the introduction of smoked salmon as an added Canadian touch.

The salmon was placed in a platter on top of finocchio leaves, decorated with pickles, capers, rounds of cut red onions and lemon slices.

We had baskets of finocchio, walnuts, hazelnuts, oranges and tangerines placed around the house, providing colour and aroma to it all.

CRUSTOLI
BAKED CABBAGE
SPAGHETTI WITH ANCHOVY SAUCE
BAKED SCALLOPS
MARINATED SEAFOOD PLATTER
ARTICHOKES
(See Section on Preserves)

BEET SALAD
BROCCOLI AND CAULIFLOWER SALAD
BROCCOLI AND CAULIFLOWER FRITTERS
LUPINI
FRIED CODFISH
TRADITIONAL COOKIES
(See Section Traditional Recipes for Scauille, Turdilli and Traditional Christmas Cake)

❖

Crustoli

This recipe is dedicated to my late brother Alberto Gallo

In the old days, the grandmother would make the dough for the crustoli and then gather the family around the fireplace. She would fry the crustoli and it was served to the children first with vino cotto. The men would have the crustoli with anchovies and red wine.

In those days, when my grandmother wanted to test if the oil was hot enough for frying, she would peel a large potato, wash and dry it well, then add it to the oil. When the potato turned golden, it meant that the oil was ready for frying.

Ingredients

6	medium potatoes, washed, cooked, mashed
2	Tbsp active dry yeast
2	tsp sugar
3	cups warm water
1	Tbsp salt
2	lbs all-purpose flour
4	bay leaves
1/2	lb anchovies
2	Tbsp hot pepper
	olive oil

Method

Dissolve sugar in 1 cup of warm water and add the yeast. Cover and set aside for about 10 minutes. Add the salt to the remaining 2 cups of water.

In the meantime, in a large dish that will allow for the doubling of the dough, add the flour. Make a well in the centre.

Add potatoes, salted water and knead with hands. Add the yeast mixture to make a soft dough. Cover with an oiled plastic sheet. Let stand for an hour away from the draught. It will be ready when it has doubled.

Fill and heat a pan with oil for deep frying.

Put anchovies in a dish. In another dish, pour one cup of oil. Dip hands in the oil and take a large pinch of dough, filling it with anchovy.

With the other hand, pull and twist dough and drop it in hot oil. When dough is golden, turn and fry on the other side. Remove from oil and drain on absorbent paper towels. ❖

Baked Cabbage

(Verza al forno)

Ingredients

6	heads Verza (curly cabbage)
1	oz olive oil
6	garlic cloves, minced
2	cups water
8	leaves mint
1	Tbsp ginger
1/2	Tbsp nutmeg
	salt to taste

Method

Cut an "X" on hard core of the cabbage and blanch for a minute in boiling water with ginger and nutmeg. Cool and chop.

Place olive oil and garlic in a large casserole with 2 cups of water. Add the chopped cabbage. Bake at 225° F for 2-3 hours. Serve. ❖

Spaghetti with Anchovy Sauce
(Spaghetti con la salsa di acciughe)

Ingredients

6-1/2	lbs spaghetti
10	cups home-made breadcrumbs
10-12	garlic cloves, minced
4	cans 1.7-oz anchovy fillets
1	cup fresh parsley, chopped
1/2	tsp savory
1/2	tsp sage
1/2	tsp thyme
2	cups olive oil

Method

This sauce can be prepared a day ahead.

Pour 1 cup of olive oil into a frying pan, adding garlic. When the garlic starts sizzling, turn off the heat. Add the remaining ingredients except spaghetti (including the other cup of oil). Keep turning until well mixed.

Cook spaghetti according to package directions. Drain spaghetti and add the sauce. Serve immediately. ❖

Baked Scallops

Ingredients

8	lbs scallops, rinsed

Marinade

1	cup wine (Verdicchio)
1	Tbsp salt
2	garlic cloves, minced
1/2	cup parsley, chopped
1/2	tsp savory
1/4	tsp thyme
1/4	tsp ginger
1/2	tsp cayenne

Method

This can be made a couple of hours ahead of time and refrigerated.

Mix all ingredients together and pour over scallops. Mix well and marinate for 2-3 hours. Refrigerate.

4	beaten eggs
3	cups breadcrumbs
1	lb butter

Preheat oven to 350° F.

Add beaten eggs to the scallops and stir. Pour melted butter into a baking dish. Roll each scallop in breadcrumbs and place into the dish.

Bake for 10 minutes. Broil for another 10 minutes. ❖

Marinated Seafood Platter

(Pescatrice, gamberi e seppie marinate)

Ingredients

9	lbs monkfish
9	lbs shrimp, washed and de-veined
2	lbs cuttlefish, washed and cleaned
10	large artichokes

Ingredients for Court Bouillon

6	cups water
2	cups dry white wine
2	large onions, chopped
2	garlic cloves
1	Tbsp salt
3	peppercorns
4	fresh sage leaves
1	tsp savory
1/2	tsp thyme
1/2	tsp rosemary
1/2	tsp tarragon
1/2	tsp dry mustard
1/4	tsp ginger

Method

Remove the dark leaves of the artichokes, peel stems and cut in half.

Combine ingredients for court bouillon in a large pot. Cover and bring to boil. Reduce heat and simmer for 5 minutes. Add artichokes and cook for 2-3 minutes until fork tender. Remove the artichokes and set aside to cool.

In the same court bouillon, add the shrimps. Simmer for one minute and remove. Set aside to cool. Add cuttlefish and cook 3-4 minutes until the colour changes. Remove and set aside to cool. Finally add monkfish and cook for 10-12 minutes.

Dressing

This dressing can be prepared a day ahead.

1/2	cup olive oil
1	lemon, juice only
1/4	cup tarragon vinegar
1/4	cup cognac

2	garlic cloves
8	sprigs parsley
1/2	tsp pepper

Method

In a blender, combine oil, lemon juice, vinegar, cognac and garlic. Blend for 5-6 seconds. Add parsley and pepper and blend for another second so that parsley will not be chopped too finely.

To serve, remove the tendons from the middle of the monkfish and cut into 1/2" slices. Arrange in the middle of two large platters.

Arrange cuttlefish and shrimp around the monkfish.

Cut artichokes into six pieces each and decorate each platter.

Pour the dressing over, turning the fish and artichokes to coat evenly.

Garnish with lemon wedges and serve cold.

Beet Salad

(Insalata di barbabietole)

Ingredients

4	cans beets or 15 medium beets, cooked

Dressing

1	oz tarragon vinegar
3	oz olive oil
1	Tbsp oregano
1/2	cup parsley, chopped
6	garlic cloves, halved
	salt to taste

Method

Mix dressing and pour over beets. Stir and serve.

Broccoli and Cauliflower Salad

(Insalata di broccoli e cavolfiore)

Ingredients

| 2 | large heads cauliflower |
| 3 | bunches broccoli |

Method

Cut an "X" on the hard core of each cauliflower. Place into boiling water with 1/2 tsp nutmeg. Cook for 3-4 minutes. Remove from water and set aside to cool.

Peel the stems of the broccoli and cut into 2 or 4 sections. Using the same boiling water, cook the broccoli for 3-4 minutes. Remove from water and set aside to cool.

Dressing

1	oz wine vinegar
2	oz olive oil
3-4	garlic cloves, halved
3-4	branches parsley, chopped
	salt to taste

Section the cauliflower and mix the broccoli in a large salad bowl. Pour dressing over and mix well. ❖

Broccoli and Cauliflower Fritters

(Frittelle di broccoli e cavolfiore)

Ingredients

| 2 | heads cooked cauliflower florets |
| 3 | bunches cooked broccoli florets |

Batter

8	eggs, beaten
3	cups flour
1/4	tsp cayenne
1/2	tsp savory
2	garlic cloves, minced
1/2	cup milk or half-and-half cream
3	bay leaves
	oil for frying
	salt to taste

Method

Mix all the ingredients together well and divide the batter in half. To half of the batter, add the cauliflower. To the other half, add the broccoli.

Heat oil with 3 bay leaves. Drop cauliflower florets about 1" apart in the hot oil. Fry on each side until golden. Drain on absorbent paper towels.

Fry the remaining half of the batter with broccoli in the same way.

Arrange the cauliflower and broccoli fritters on both halves of a serving platter. ❖

Lupini

(Lupini)

Lupini are usually served at Christmas, but are also excellent as a snack any time.

Ingredients

2	lbs dried lupini (1 large bag)
2	64-oz jars or 4 32-oz jars
3-1/2	pints of water
2	Tbsp salt

Method

Soak overnight in 3-4 times the amount of water to cover. The next day, boil in a large pot of water until tender. Drain water and soak again, changing the water 3-4 times a day, until sweet.

Boil water and salt for 1-2 minutes. Fill sterilized jars with drained lupini and add boiling salted water. Seal with new lids. They will keep for 3-4 months.

To Serve

Drain lupini from jar. Rinse and put into a small salad bowl. Serve plain or with this dressing.

Dressing

1/2	oz wine vinegar
1	tsp oregano
1	Tbsp olive oil

Mix and serve. ❖

Fried Codfish

(Baccalà fritto)

Ingredients

52	pieces codfish, approx. 4 oz each
1	lb black olives
2	lemons, cut in wedges
5-6	branches parsley

Marinade

1	cup Verdicchio or any dry white wine
2	garlic cloves
1/2	tsp tarragon
1/2	tsp savory
1/2	tsp sage
5	branches parsley
1	Tbsp salt
2	cups all-purpose flour
	enough olive oil for frying

Method

The marinade can be prepared the night before.

In a blender, combine all marinade ingredients. Pour over fish and stir well. Refrigerate.

When ready to use, drain fish in a colander. Cover a large area on a counter with freezer paper or aluminum paper.

Pour the flour onto the paper and coat each piece of fish well. Place each piece separately prior to frying. Heat oil and fry codfish pieces 1" apart until golden on both sides. Place individually on absorbent paper towels.

Place black olives in same hot oil and fry until they plump up. Remove with slotted spoon.

In a large serving dish, arrange codfish over the parsley branches. Garnish with black olives and lemon wedges. ❖

New Year's Eve Dinner Menu

Serves 25

To the Italians, New Year's Eve is very significant, and it is important to start the year right. That's why we kick it off with a feast such as this. The New Year's Eve Day that we prepared this feast was such a lovely sunny day that we decided to barbecue the goose.

LENTIL SOUP

CANADIAN GOOSE

GREEN MANICOTTI

CROWN ROAST

STEAMED COLLARDS

MIXED SALAD

APPLE AND PUMPKIN PIE

ST. JOHNS HERBAL TEA

Lentil Soup
(Zuppa di lenticchie)

This is a great New Year's Eve soup which Italians think brings great wealth and happiness. It was a staple with the Egyptians, Greeks and Romans, and has been used since Biblical times. It is usually served at a buffet for good luck.

Lentils are a valuable source of vitamin B, iron and phosphorous. It is inexpensive and takes very little time to prepare. You can prepare it in the morning, go to work and leave it in a crockpot or cook it over a stove. But the best flavour, I find, comes from cooking it in the oven.

You can double the ingredients and keep any extra refrigerated up to a week. Just bring the leftovers to boil and sprinkle parmiggiano on top for a different flavour. Any vegetable can be added for a different taste - leek, broccoli, turnips or potato, chopped. Mix it with cooked pasta, boiled and drained according to package instructions.

Ingredients

2	lbs lentils
5	cups water
1	tomato
2	slices yellow pumpkin or potatoes
2	onions chopped
1	garlic clove, chopped
1	stalk celery, chopped
2	Tbsp parsley, minced
2	bay leaves
1	piece ginger, about 1"

Method

Rinse lentils with warm water. Place in pot, add water to cover and bring to boil.

Place all vegetables and spices in a casserole dish. Add lentils and the water you cooked them in. Cover and cook in preheated oven at 250° F for 2 hours.

If you prefer, cook over the stove. This is faster but takes more water, so remember to double the amount of water to be used.

Soak for 1 hour before cooking for 1 hour.

Canadian Goose

(Oca alla canadese)

Ingredients

2	6-lb geese
2	lemons
	salt and pepper

Method

A day before cooking, trim fat and keep for later use. Rinse geese with cold water. Drain well and pat dry. Rub the lemon inside and outside each goose. Sprinkle with salt and pepper, and rub well.

Broth

2	goose necks
12	cups water
1	celery stalk
1	garlic clove
2	sage leaves
4	juniper berries
1	peppercorn
	salt to taste

A day before cooking geese, in a saucepan, bring to boil goose neck and 12 cups water. Skim, then combine all ingredients. Reduce heat, cover and simmer for 1-1/2 hours. When cool, cover and refrigerate until ready for use.

Stuffing

	gizzard, liver, heart, finely chopped
1/4	cup butter
1	lb pork fillet (cut into 20 pieces)
3	garlic cloves
2	oz porcini mushrooms, dried
4	oz sparkling Martini
1	lb Canadian wild rice
1	tsp dry sage
1	tsp thyme
4	branches parsley
10	dry apricots
2	oz pine nuts
2	eggs, slightly beaten

Method

Rinse mushrooms and keep in hot water. Squeeze when ready to use.

Melt butter in large heavy skillet over medium heat. Add meat, gizzard, liver, heart, garlic and mushrooms. Sauté for 2-3 minutes.

Add 2 oz wine and cook for 1 minute. Add rice, one cup of broth and stir until broth has evaporated. Remove from heat.

Add herbs, pine nuts, apricots and remaining wine. Cool. Add beaten eggs.

Divide stuffing into two and fill goose cavities.

Ingredients for Roasting Pan

2	cups broth
2	celery stalks
2	bay leaves
2	red peppercorns
1	bunch parsley
4	garlic cloves
1	branch savory
1	branch thyme
1	branch rosemary

Place all ingredients in a roasting pan. Place geese breasts down on top of herbs. Cover with foil and grill over a coal barbecue. Allow 15 minutes for each 1 lb. Every 15 minutes, baste geese with broth. When geese are cooked, remove and set aside to cool. Remove stuffing onto a platter. Carve and serve. ❖

Green Manicotti

(Manicotti verdi)

This recipe makes 48 manicotti, which is ideal if you are serving 2 dozen guests 2 each. You can still make this quantity ahead of time and freeze the manicotti for later use. This is enough for 3 dinners for a family of 6. I like to make the sauce fresh on the day I'm serving it, but you can vary the sauce you are serving it with.

Crêpe Ingredients

3	cups all-purpose flour
1/2	lb spinach, washed, cut, steamed
8	eggs
3	cups milk
1/4	lb butter
1	tsp salt

Method

Place spinach and eggs in a blender and blend for 1-2 minutes. Turn into a bowl and add remaining ingredients. Whisk until a smooth, runny consistency is reached. Let rest for at least 1/2 hour.

Ladle a serving spoonful into a non-stick crêpe pan. Turn over high heat and flip over. Continue until batter is finished.

Filling

2	lbs lean beef, minced
2	lbs lean pork, minced
2	lbs veal, minced
2	garlic cloves
4	green onions, white part, chopped
1/2	cup dry white wine
1/4	tsp nutmeg
5	sprigs parsley
2	cups breadcrumbs
2	cups parmiggiano
2	eggs, slightly beaten
2	oz oil
	salt and pepper to taste

Method

In a pan, put oil, onions, meat and garlic. Cook covered over low heat for 10 minutes, stirring occasionally.

Remove cover and continue cooking until liquid has evaporated.

Add wine, parsley, salt, pepper, nutmeg, breadcrumbs and cheese. Stir. When cool, add eggs and stir well.

Take a crêpe in the palm of your hand. Fill with about 2 Tbsp stuffing. Then gently roll it and place in baking casserole. Continue until all crêpes are filled.

Sauce

2	lbs shoulder goat meat, cleaned and cut into pieces
6	garlic cloves, minced
4	onions, white part, minced
4	sage leaves
2	tsp fresh savory
1	cup dry white wine
6	sprigs parsley, minced
2	oz oil
2	lbs mozzarella, grated
6	26-oz cans tomatoes, peeled and strained
2	cups parmiggiano
	salt and pepper to taste

Method

Place oil in a pan. Over low heat, add onions, garlic and meat. Cook covered for 10 minutes, stirring occasionally. Remove cover and add wine, cooking until meat browns. Add tomatoes. Bring to boil and simmer for 1/2 hour.

Add parsley, sage, savory, salt and pepper. Stir.

Ladle sauce over manicotti. Grate mozzarella over the manicotti. Sprinkle parmiggiano over. Cover with foil. Bake at 350° F for 30-40 minutes. ❖

Crown Roast

(Arrosto di maiale al gin)

This is my brother-in-law, Joseph Bumbaca's super-favourite crown roast.

Ingredients

1	crown roast with a dozen ribs
1	cup gin
3	oz olive oil
1	fresh ginger (2''), sliced
1/2	tsp sage
1/2	tsp black pepper
1/2	tsp hyssop
1/2	tsp hot pepper
1/2	tsp fennel seeds
6	branches parsley
6	cooking apples, cored, peeled and halved
1	Tbsp salt

Place parsley at the bottom and crown roast in a roasting pan. Pour in oil and gin. Rub all herbs and spices into and all over the meat. Cover and refrigerate overnight.

Preheat the oven to 400° F.

Rub marinade into meat again before baking.

Bake covered with foil paper for 10 minute. Reduce heat to 350° F and allow 20 minutes per lb.

Meatball Stuffing

2	lbs minced meat from crown roast, unspiced
2	eggs
1/2	cup wheatgerm
1/4	cup gin
3	branches chervil, minced
2	branches caraway, minced
	salt and pepper to taste

Method

In a dish, mix all ingredients with your hands. Mould into medium-sized meatballs.

An hour before the roast is done, add meatballs inside the crown and apples around the roast.

When the roast is done, take it out of the oven and pour the rest of the gin over.

With a slotted spoon, remove apples and meatballs. Place roast in centre of serving dish, and arrange apples and meatballs around it. Sieve the herbs from the juice and remove any unwanted fat.

Slice crown roast, dip into juice and serve. Decorate serving dish with caraway branches.   ❖

Steamed Collards

(Cavolini lessi)

Ingredients

2	bunches collards
1/4	tsp ginger
1/4	tsp nutmeg
3	oz goose fat
2	garlic cloves
1	onion, chopped
1/2	tsp fennel seeds
	salt and pepper to taste

Method

Place water, nutmeg, ginger and salt in a pot and bring to boil. Blanch collards. Remove from burner and place collards in colander to cool. Cut into quarters.

In a casserole, place fat, garlic, onions, salt and pepper. Sauté for 2 minutes. Add collards, fennel seeds and cover. Cook for at least 20 minutes. ❖

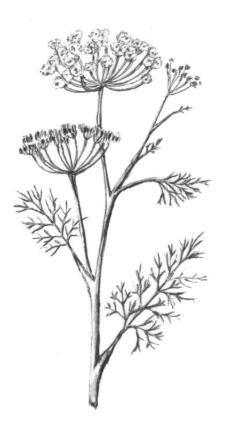

Mixed Salad

(Insalata Mista)

Ingredients

2	heads romaine lettuce
3	heads radicchio
2	medium cucumbers
1	bunch rucola
2	heads curly endives
5	heads Belgian lettuce
2	large cooking apples
1/2	cup mint, chopped
2	small green onions, cut very fine

Dressing

1	cup olive oil
1/2	cup raspberry vinegar
1	Tbsp oregano
1	garlic clove, crushed

Method

Wash and cut salad greens. Core and chop apples.

Place all dressing ingredients in a jar and shake well. Place salad ingredients in a salad bowl. Just before serving, shake dressing well.
Pour over salad, mix
well and serve. ❖

Apple and Pumpkin Pie
(Torta di zuccha alle mele)

This is my second son, Domenico's favourite recipe.

Crust

4	cups flour
2	Tbsp sugar
1	tsp salt
1/2	tsp cinnamon
2	oz coconut
2	oz almonds, crushed
1-1/2	cup shortening
1/2	cup cold water
1	egg, slightly beaten
1	Tbsp white vinegar

Method

The crust can be prepared a day ahead.

Measure dry ingredients into a medium-sized bowl. Cut into shortening with a pastry blender until mixture is crumbly.

In a glass, mix all liquid ingredients. Add liquid ingredients to dry, mixing until dough clings together. Refrigerate for at least an hour.

Roll out on a lightly floured surface big enough to fit a 4 quart casserole. Cut pastry 1/4" larger than the 10-1/2" x 15" x 2-1/4" dish. Fold under and pinch edges.

Filling

2	cups canned pumpkin
2	eggs
1	cup milk or half-and-half
1-1/4	cup brown sugar
1/2	tsp salt
1/2	tsp cinnamon
1/4	tsp mace
1/4	tsp ginger
1/4	tsp nutmeg
1/4	tsp clove

Method

In a blender, blend milk, spices, eggs and sugar for one minute. Turn into a medium-sized bowl. Add pumpkin and stir well. Pour into prepared shell.

Topping

5	cooking apples, cut into wedges
2	Tbsp brown sugar
3	oz apricot brandy

Method

In a frying pan, add brandy and sugar. Stir well. Add apples and cook over medium heat for 5 minutes. Cool slightly.

Arrange topping over filling in an attractive design.

Bake at 450° F for 5 minutes. Lower heat to 350° F and bake for 40-45 minutes until set. ❖

St. John's Herbal Tea
(Tisana di San Giovanni)

Serves 8

Ingredients

1/2	cup St. John's Wort
4	cardamom seeds, crushed
2	bay leaves
2	Tbsp angelica

Method

Place all ingredients in a covered saucepan. Bring to boil. Turn off heat and let stand for 10-15 minutes. Serve with honey or brown sugar.

For large parties, make 3 pots of tea. ❖

Businessmen's Delight Menu

(Delizia per uomini d'affari)

Serves 6

This is a favourite menu for entertaining my husband's business associates and guests.

FLORAL BORAGE DIP WITH APRICOT BRANDY

VEGETABLE BASKET

SIRLOIN MARINATED WITH JUNIPER AND TARRAGON

ASPARAGUS WITH MINT OR PARSLEY SAUCE

POTATO SURPRISE

ENDIVE SALAD

APPLE PIE PARFAIT

Floral Borage Dip with Apricot Brandy

(Fiore di borraggine "dip" al brandy di albicocche)

Ingredients

1	lb cream cheese, at room temperature
1	oz blue cheese, at room temperature
1	Tbsp mayonnaise
2	oz apricot brandy
30	borage flowers

Method

In a blender, blend the first 4 ingredients. Add borage flowers and stir. Reserve few flowers to sprinkle on top of dip. ❖

Vegetable Basket

Ingredients

4	carrots, cut lengthwise
4	celery stalks, cut lengthwise
1	green pepper, cut lengthwise
1	red pepper, cut lengthwise
10	cherry tomatoes
8	green onions
8	radishes, cut into florets
1	small head cauliflower, cut into florets
2	tarragon branches
2	savory branches
4	sage branches

Method

Decorate a basket with tarragon branches, sage and savory. Place dip in the middle of the basket. Accompany with crisp raw vegetables. ❖

Sirloin Marinated with Juniper and Tarragon

(Filetto di manzo con cipresso e dragoncello)

Ingredients

2	lbs sirloin, cut 2-1/2" thick
1/2	cup white wine
3	branches tarragon, chopped
1/4	tsp fresh grated ginger
15	juniper berries, crushed
1/4	tsp sweet pepper
1/4	tsp oregano
	salt and pepper to taste

Method

Place meat in a dish, add all ingredients and marinate for 3 hours.

Grill over barbecue to your liking. ❖

Asparagus with Mint or Parsley Sauce
(Asparaci con salsa di menta)

You can choose either the mint or the parsley sauce to go with the asparagus.

Ingredients

2	bunches asparagus

Method

Cut darker parts of asparagus and save for soup. Soak in salt water for 1/2 an hour. Rinse well. Tie asparagus with string and place in boiling water with tips up. Cook for 2-3 minutes until tender. Drain and place in a serving dish.

Mint Sauce

2	Tbsp olive oil
1	garlic clove
1/2	oz tarragon vinegar
1/2	cup fresh mint leaves, chopped
2	Tbsp breadcrumbs
10	mint leaves for decoration
	Juice of 1/2 lemon

Method

In a blender, blend lemon juice and all other ingredients, except mint leaves, for 1 minute. Add mint leaves and mix well. Pour over asparagus. Sprinkle with breadcrumbs. Decorate with mint leaves.

Parsley Sauce

This may also be prepared a day ahead and refrigerated, or you can make slightly more and refrigerate for later use. This keeps well if you add a tablespoonful of oil over the top. Store in a glass jar.

2	bunches parsley
2	oz olive oil
1	tsp crushed red pepper
	salt and pepper to taste

Method

Wash parsley and dry very well. In a blender, mix the oil alternately with parsley leaves. Blend until creamy.

Store in a jar and cover with a teaspoon of oil. Cover tightly. Refrigerate for later use. ❖

Potato Surprise
(Patate alla sorpresa)

Ingredients

6	medium potatoes, washed and peeled
1	red pepper, julienned
1	zucchini
4	green onions, chopped
3	garlic cloves, minced
20	chives, chopped
1	Tbsp rosemary, crushed
2	oz olive oil
1/4	tsp cayenne
1/2	tsp paprika
	salt to taste

Method

Preheat the oven to 400° F.

Slice potatoes into thin rounds and cut zucchini in the same way. In a 13" x 9" x 2" casserole dish, add the oil and the rest of the ingredients. Mix with your hands and pat down. Cover dish with foil.

Bake at 400° F for 10 minutes, then turn down heat to 300° F and bake for 1/2 hour or until fork-tender.

When ready to serve, divide into squares.

Endive Salad

(Insalata di indivia)

Ingredients

2	heads endive, washed and cut
4	white radishes sliced
2	carrots, shredded
2	Tbsp raisins
1	cooking apple thinly sliced

Dressing

	juice of 1/2 lemon
1	oz olive oil
1	garlic clove, crushed
10	mint leaves, chopped
1/2	tsp summer savory
1/2	oz tarragon wine vinegar
	salt and pepper to taste

Mix the dressing ingredients together and pour over the endive salad. Toss and serve. ❖

Apple Pie Parfait

(Torta di mele perfetto)

Crust

4	cups flour
2	Tbsp sugar
1	tsp salt
1/2	tsp cinnamon
2	oz coconut
2	oz almonds, crushed
1-1/2	cup shortening
1/2	cup cold water
1	egg, slightly beaten
1	Tbsp white vinegar
1	Tbsp brown sugar for top of pie
2	Tbsp milk for top of pie

Method

The crust can be prepared a day ahead.

Measure dry ingredients into a medium-sized bowl. Cut into shortening with a pastry blender until mixture is crumbly.

In a glass, mix all liquid ingredients. Add liquid ingredients to dry, mixing until dough clings together. Divide dough into two and refrigerate for at least an hour.

Roll out on a lightly floured surface big enough for a pie dish. Cut pastry 1/4" larger than pie dish. Pack filling inside the pie dish. Place pastry over, fold over and seal. With a fork, make designs in top of crust. Brush milk over pie and sprinkle with brown sugar.

Filling

8	medium apples, peeled, and quartered
1/2	cup brown sugar
2	Tbsp honey
2	Tbsp oat bran
1/4	cup almonds, finely ground
2	Tbsp amaretto
1/2	tsp cinnamon
1/4	tsp ground cloves

Method

Preheat oven to 450° F.

Combine all ingredients in a bowl and toss. Leave for an hour.

Bake at 450° F for 8 minutes, then reduce heat to 350° F and bake for 30-35 minutes. ❖

Summer Menu

(Menù d'estate)

Serves 6

This is a great menu for entertaining on a lazy Saturday, when you don't want to be doing a lot of cooking. Once in a while, my husband Federico gives me a day off and cooks instead. This menu features his speciality, which I have affectionately called "Federico's Sea Bass".

FEDERICO'S SEA BASS

RICE AND SPINACH

ASPARAGUS WITH PEAS

GREEN SALAD

GRAPES IN COINTREAU

Federico's Sea Bass

(Spigola alla Federico)

Ingredients

4	lbs fresh sea bass
2	cups water
1/2	cup white wine
5	bay leaves
5	cloves
6	juniper berries
4	sage leaves
1/2	tsp thyme
	salt and pepper to taste

Dressing

1/2	cup white wine
3	Tbsp parsley, minced
2	Tbsp olive oil
1	garlic clove, minced
	juice of 1/2 lemon
	salt and pepper to taste

Method

Preheat oven to 300° F.

Prepare a roasting pan with a rack. Place all ingredients except sea bass, salt and pepper in the roasting pan.

Clean sea bass and season with salt and pepper to taste. Place on rack and broil it for 30 minutes on each side.

Meanwhile, in a small bowl, add all dressing ingredients. Mix well.

When fish is cooked, de-bone it and place in a warm platter. Spoon dressing over. Decorate with lemon wedges and parsley. ❖

Rice and Spinach

(Riso con spinaci)

Ingredients

3	cups rice
1	Tbsp butter
2	garlic cloves, minced
1	lb spinach

Rinse rice and place in a medium-sized pot. Wash and chop spinach and place on top of rice. Add garlic, butter and cover with water. Bring to boil over medium heat. Stir well. Turn off heat and leave covered on burner. The residual heat will cook the rice. ❖

Asparagus with Peas

(Asparaci con piselli)

Ingredients

1	garlic clove, chopped
4	green onions, chopped
2	bunches asparagus, cut
8	oz frozen peas
1/2	cup water or chicken broth
1/4	cup olive oil or butter

Method

Cover the bottom of a pan with olive oil or butter. Add garlic, onions, asparagus and peas. Shake, cover and cook over medium heat for 5-10 minutes or until asparagus is tender. Add salt to taste. ❖

Green Salad

(Insalata verde)

Ingredients

1	head Boston lettuce
2	heads curly escarole
2	radishes, sliced
1	green onion, chopped
3	Tbsp fresh garlic chives, chopped
1	Tbsp tarragon

Dressing

2	oz olive oil
1	oz tarragon vinegar
1/2	tsp oregano

Method

Rinse and cut lettuce. Place all salad ingredients in a salad bowl.

In a jar, shake all dressing ingredients well and pour over salad before serving. ❖

Grapes in Cointreau

(Uva al cointreau)

Ingredients

3	cups seedless white grapes
1/2	cup Cointreau
	rind and juice of 1 orange
6	leaves pineapple sage

Method

Wash grapes. Place in a dish. Mix with rest of ingredients except pineapple sage. Serve in cocktail glasses. Decorate each glass with a leaf of pineapple sage. ❖

Summer Seafood Dinner

(Serata d'estate - frutti di mare)

Serves 6

OYSTERS

BLACK RADISH SAUCE

BARBECUED SWORDFISH

CAULIFLOWER WITH RICE

STEAMED ESCAROLE

BLUEBERRY-PEACH PIE

Oysters
(Ostriche)

To open an oyster, I just tickle it on the back with the point of a knife and pry the shell sideways. Hey presto! I've got it opened and I can now open an oyster shell per second.

Ingredients

2	doz oysters
1	lemon, cut in wedges
7	sprigs parsley
	crushed ice

Method

Cover bottom of a large serving dish with crushed ice and arrange oysters with lemon wedges and sprigs of parsley around. Serve as an antipasto with white wine or champagne. ❖

Black Radish Sauce
(Salsa di ravanello nero)

Ingredients

1	black radish, grated
1/4	cup raspberry vinegar
2	Tbsp olive oil
2	Tbsp parsley, minced
2	Tbsp fresh dill
	salt and white pepper to taste

Method

In a large dish, add black grated radish and raspberry vinegar. Cover for 1/2 hour. Drain and add remaining ingredients.

Serve with smoked salmon, oysters or smoked sturgeon. It goes very well with rye bread. ❖

Barbecued Swordfish
(Pesce spada alla griglia)

Ingredients

3	1" swordfish steaks, divided in half
1/2	cup white wine

Rinse the swordfish steaks with white wine.
In a blender, add the following:

1	oz white wine
1	garlic clove
4	leaves chervil
2	leaves caraway
5	sprigs parsley
1/2	Tbsp olive oil
	juice of 1/2 lime

Pour blender mixture over fish, turn and let stand until ready to barbecue.

Make sure the barbecue is very hot. Cook the swordfish steaks for 4 minutes on each side. Do not overcook.

Serve on a large platter garnished with chervil leaves and limes. ❖

Cauliflower with Rice
(Cavolfiore con riso)

Ingredients

1/2	head cauliflower, washed and chopped
3	cups rice, rinsed
2	Tbsp butter
1	garlic clove
15	sprigs parsley
2	Tbsp parmiggiano
	salt to taste

Method

In a pot add all the ingredients except the parmiggiano. Cover with water and bring to boil. Stir and lower heat to simmer. Cook covered for approx. 10 minutes until rice is cooked.

Place in serving dish and sprinkle with parmiggiano.

Steamed Escarole

Ingredients

2	bunches escarole
1/2	cup water
1/4	oz olive oil
2	garlic cloves, minced
2	onions, sliced
1	hot pepper, optional
	salt and pepper to taste

Method

Rinse escarole and cut in two. Place all ingredients in a pan. Cover and cook on low heat for 20-25 minutes.

Also can be served mixed with rice or with pasta. ❖

Blueberry-Peach Pie

(Crostata di mirtilli e pesche)

Crust

2	cups all-purpose flour
1	Tbsp brown sugar
1/2	Tbsp salt
1/4	tsp cinnamon
1	oz coconut, dessicated
1	oz pecans, ground
3/4	cup shortening
1/4	cup cold water
1	egg, slightly beaten
1/2	Tbsp vinegar
10	leaves verbena, minced

Method

Mix together the water, egg and vinegar in a measuring cup. Stir together the dry ingredients. Cut in the shortening with a pastry blender until the pieces are pea-sized.

Add the liquids and push gently with a fork. Repeat until moistened and it forms a ball. Refrigerate until ready for use.

Filling

1-1/2	pints blueberries, washed and drained
2	medium peaches
1	Tbsp cornstarch
1/4	tsp cinnamon
1	Tbsp almonds, minced
1/2	lemon, grated
2	Tbsp lemon juice
1/2	cup brown sugar
1	oz cherry brandy
1	Tbsp unflavoured gelatine

Method

Preheat oven to 400° F.

Mix all ingredients in a large bowl and sprinkle the gelatine over the mixture.

Take the ball of dough and flatten on a lightly floured surface. Roll from centre to outside in a rectangular shape to fit a rectangular dish. Pour filling into pie crust. Turn overhanging dough under the rim to form a narrow roll. Flute the edges and bake at 400° F for 5 minutes. Reduce heat to 350° F and bake for 40-45 minutes or until crust is light golden brown. ❖

The Feast after the Fashion Show

Serves 50

The year my youngest son Leonardo enrolled at Leonardo da Vinci School (a private school), I organized a hair styling and fashion show at the Old Mill with the help of other mothers.

The show was attended by more than 300 guests, and the funds raised were donated to the school.

After the show, I had more than 50 people, both models and guests, at my house for a buffet supper. It was a tremendous success.

EGGPLANT DIP

VEGETABLE BASKET
(See Business Men's Delight - Double the recipe)

ANCHOVIES WITH CAPERS

VEAL TONGUE AND HEART IN GELATINE

HOT OR SWEET SAUSAGE
(See Traditional Recipes - Use half of the recipe)

MUSHROOM AND ARTICHOKE SALAD

CHICKEN BREAST DELIGHT

EGGPLANT TIELLA
(See Federico's 50th Birthday Menu)

POLENTA
(See Menu for Six - Double the recipe)

A LITTLE MORE THAN DATE SQUARES

TIRAMISÙ

RED AND WHITE WINE

Eggplant Dip

Ingredients

1	large eggplant
2	garlic cloves
1/2	cup pine nuts
2	oz olive oil
1/2	tsp savory
1/2	tsp marjoram
1/2	tsp hyssop
1/2	tsp thyme
	juice of 1 lemon
	salt and pepper to taste

Method

Wash eggplant and place in a dish. Bake at 300° F for an hour or until tender. Cool before peeling. Remove seeds by passing eggplant through a sieve.

Place all ingredients in a blender for 1 minute.

Serve with raw vegetables or cold meats.

Anchovies with Capers

Ingredients

1	1-lb can anchovies in oil
1	1/2-lb can capers
6	hot peppers (red and green cut lengthwise)
1	cup fresh caraway or parsley
2	Tbsp raspberry vinegar
1/4	cup virgin olive oil
1/2	cup white wine

Method

Drain oil from anchovies. Rinse with white wine. Squeeze oil out.

Rinse capers with cold water. Squeeze tight.

Wash caraway and dry well with absorbent paper towel.

In a serving dish, layer caraway leaves on the bottom, top with anchovies and finally with capers and hot peppers. Repeat layers. Drizzle oil and vinegar evenly over the top.

Press a piece of waxed paper over the top and refrigerate. This can keep at least a week refrigerated.

Serve at room temperature.

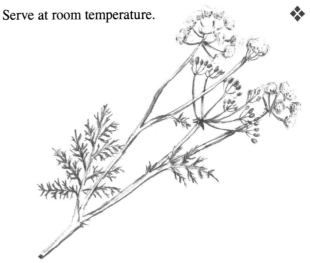

Veal Tongue and Heart in Gelatine

(Gelatina di lingua e cuore di vitello)

Ingredients

5	lbs veal heart
3-1/2	lbs veal tongue
3	pig's trotters
8	pints water
1	onion, peeled
2	garlic cloves
2	bay leaves
1	piece ginger 1", peeled
2	little hot peppers
1/2	tsp coriander
4	cloves
1/2	tsp cumin
1	cup white vinegar

Method

Wash trotters. Cover heart and trotters with cold water. Let stand for 1/2 hour. Place tongue in pan. Cover with water and bring to a boil. Cook for 2 minutes. Remove from burner. Drain and cover with cold water. Remove white film from tongue and trim fat.

In a pan, place all ingredients except vinegar. Cook over medium heat until fork-tender. Remove heart and tongue with a slotted spoon. Trim nerves from heart. Slice heart and tongue and place in a serving dish.

Continue to boil remaining ingredients for 20 minutes. Sieve liquid and reserve 2 cups. Add 1 cup of vinegar to the 2 cups, bring to boil in a pan. Turn heat off.

Take 1/2 cup of liquid and pour slowly over heart and tongue until covered. Place a couple of dishes over to weigh it down. Repeat process. Let stand until liquid has cooled. Refrigerate. Serve the next day.

The pig's trotters may also be sliced and served as a side dish.

Mushroom and Artichoke Salad

(Insalata di funghi e carciofi)

Ingredients

2	lbs mushrooms, cleaned and halved
12	artichokes, cleaned and quartered

In a large pan, combine the following and bring to boil:

4	cups water
2	cups white vinegar
2	Tbsp salt
2	leaves sage
2	bay leaves
1/2	tsp hot pepper

Method

Add artichokes to boiling liquid. When fork-tender, remove and place in a colander. Cover with dish.

In the same boiling liquid add mushrooms. Leave them for about 1 minute, then remove with slotted spoon and drain in a colander.

Dressing

1	heart of celery, cut in style with leaves
1/2	cup olive oil
3	garlic cloves, halved
2	Tbsp raspberry vinegar
1	tsp marjoram

Mix dressing ingredients well.

Toss like a salad. Arrange in a serving dish with celery leaves.

Canadian Goose
Recipe page 133

Cauliflower and Tomato Salad
Recipe page 64

1. *Black Aniseed* 2. *Aniseed* 3. *Myrrh Raisins* 4. *Cardamom* 5. *Chili Pepper* 6. *Hot Cherry Pepper*
7. *Cayenne* 8. *Hot Pepper Seeds* 9. *Black Pepper* 10. *Paprika* 11. *Juniper* 12. *Sea Salt* 13. *Curry Flower*
14. *Saffron* 15. *Curry* 16. *Turmeric* 17. *Ginger* 18. *Mustard Seeds* 19. *Coriander (in centre of plate of Mustard*
Seeds) 20. *Cumin* 21. *Caraway* 22. *Clove* 23. *Nutmeg* 24. *Thyme* 25. *Fennel* 26. *Allspice* 27. *Cinnamon*

Chicken Breast Delight

(Petto di pollo alla delizia)

Ingredients

20	pieces chicken breast, quartered
4	eggs, slightly beaten
2	oz sherry
4	cups breadcrumbs
1/2	cup parmiggiano
1/2	tsp curry
1/2	tsp turmeric
1/2	tsp nutmeg
2	Tbsp parsley, minced
1/2	tsp savory
1/2	tsp cayenne
1/2	tsp freshly ground pepper
2	garlic cloves
2	cups olive oil
	salt to taste

Method

Rinse the meat with cold water and place in a colander. Sprinkle salt, pepper, cayenne and ginger. Let stand for 5 minutes.

In a big dish, add chicken, eggs, sherry, turmeric, nutmeg, parsley, savory and garlic. Mix, cover and refrigerate till ready to cook.

Place breadcrumbs and parmiggiano on a piece of waxed paper, and mix together with your hands.

Coat the chicken individually in the breadcrumb and cheese mixture and place separately on another piece of waxed paper. Do not overlap.

Pour enough oil in a frying pan for deep frying. Fry chicken until light-golden. Then place in a baking dish and bake in oven at 300° F for 10-15 minutes.

Serve with steamed rice and candied fruit. ❖

A Little More than Date Squares

Makes 24-2" squares

Ingredients
Filling

5	cups dates, chopped
1-1/2	cups maple syrup
1	cup vermouth
1	tsp vanilla
1	lemon rind
4	Tbsp lemon juice
10	cardamom seeds, crushed

Crust

1-1/2	cups unsalted butter, melted
2-1/2	cups all-purpose flour
2-1/2	cups lightly packed brown sugar
2-1/2	cups rolled oats
1	tsp baking soda

Method

Preheat oven to 325° F (160° C). Grease 9" x 13" x 2" baking pan.

In a saucepan, combine all ingredients for filling. Simmer until thickened. Set aside to cool. The filling can be prepared ahead and refrigerated up to one week. If storing it, cover the surface with plastic wrap. When ready to use, bring to room temperature.

Meanwhile, mix all ingredients for crust with a fork. Press half of crumb mixture into baking pan. Spread with cool date mixture. Add remaining crumb mixture and press down firmly.

Bake for 30 minutes until golden brown. Let cool and wrap in wax paper, then foil. Store in refrigerator and when cold, cut into squares. They also freeze well. ❖

Tiramisù

For the fashion show, my sister Rosa contributed a dessert (Tiramisù), which was absolutely heavenly. The secret to this recipe is to use fresh eggs, fresh mascarpone cheese, round biscuits and dry Savoiardi cookies (which you can buy from any Italian store).

We also make our own vanilla sugar by adding 4-5 vanilla beans to 2 lb of sugar, and leave it in a glass jar for use when required. If you don't have vanilla sugar, add 3 Tbsp of pure vanilla to sugar.

Ingredients

2	cups expresso coffee
2	Tbsp cocoa
1-1/2	cups Kahlua
18	Tbsp vanilla sugar
16	eggs, separated
1/4	tsp salt
48	dry Savoiardi cookies
18	round biscuits
2	lbs mascarpone (2 packages)

Method

In a wide dish, mix coffee and Kahlua liqueur. In a bowl, beat sugar and yolks at medium speed for 6-7 minutes until they are pale. Add mascarpone and blend by hand.

In another bowl, beat egg whites and salt until peaks are formed. Fold white mixture into mascarpone mixture until creamy.

Quickly dip Savoiardi biscuits in the coffee mixture and cover the bottom of a large china tray. Spoon 1" of the creamy mixture over the top and smooth with spatula.

Continue second layer by dipping Savoiardi biscuits with coffee mixture, then topping with creamy mixture. Continue until everything is finished and the creamy mixture is like a glaze all over. Arrange the round biscuits around the cake.

Sift cocoa over the top. Refrigerate for at least 4 hours.

Serve when ready.

Palm Sunday Menu

Serves 25

STUFFED MANICOTTI WITH
MUSHROOMS AND FRESH HERBS

CHEESE SAUCE

SPRING TURKEY

RITA'S STUFFING, VODKA STUFFING,
ITALIAN RICE STUFFING, CRANBERRY SAUCE

LAMB OR GOAT TIELLA

GREEN BEANS AND CAULIFLOWER SALAD
(See Section on Vegetables)

MARINATED MUSHROOMS AND CAPERS

GREEN SALAD

EASTER BREAD

LAMB OR GOAT TIELLA

CECILIA'S CHOCOLATE CHEESECAKE

RED AND WHITE WINE

COFFEE

Stuffed Manicotti with Mushrooms and Fresh Herbs

(Ripieno di manicotti ai funghi con erbe fresche)

Makes 45 manicotti

Ingredients for Crèpes

8	eggs
1	lb all-purpose flour
1	tsp salt
1/4	butter, melted
3	cups milk

Method

Blend all ingredients for a minute or two. Turn into a bowl and add remaining ingredients. Whisk until a smooth, runny consistency is reached. Let rest for at least 1 hour.

Ladle a serving spoonful into a non-stick crèpe pan. Turn over high heat and flip over. This makes 45 manicotti.

Filling

1/2	cup unsalted butter
1	garlic clove, minced
3	lbs mushrooms, rinsed, cleaned and finely shredded
1	cup walnuts, grated
2	cups breadcrumbs
1-1/2	cups borage or spinach, minced
2	Tbsp hyssop
1/2	cup parsley
2	Tbsp fresh savory
1	Tbsp fresh tarragon
1	oz rum
1/2	Tbsp nutmeg, freshly ground
2	lbs ricotta (2 packages)

Ingredients for Topping

1	cup grated fontina cheese
1	cup grated parmiggiano cheese

Sauté butter, garlic and mushrooms over high heat for 5 minutes. Stir sonstantly. Remove from burner. Add nuts, breadcrumbs and herbs.

When cool, add ricotta, rum, nutmeg, salt and pepper. Mix well. Spoon onto manicotti, and roll. Place in oven-proof casserole.

Place the following white sauce (Cheese Sauce), along with fontina cheese and parmiggiano cheese, on top of the manicotti.

Preheat oven to 350° F. Bake for about 1/2 hour or until cheese has melted. ❖

Cheese Sauce

(Salsa bianca con due formaggi)

Ingredients

6	cups cold milk
1/4	cups butter, unsalted
1/4	cup all-purpose flour
1	cup fontina cheese, grated
1	cup parmiggiano cheese, grated
1/2	tsp nutmeg
1	Tbsp butter for topping
	salt and pepper to taste

Method

In a heavy pan, place butter and flour over low heat, stirring constantly until light golden. Add milk and keep stirring until creamy.

Add cheeses, nutmeg, salt and pepper. Stir until blended. As soon as the cheese has melted, remove from stove.

Place sauce in a container. Place 1 Tbsp of butter on top. Cover with plastic wrap and refrigerate until ready to serve.

This sauce is also delicious for asparagus, cauliflower or broccoli. ❖

Spring Turkey

(Tacchino alla primavera)

Turkey is one of my favourite meats and I cook it three or four times a year; at Thanksgiving, Christmas, Easter and for special occasions. I take pride in cooking turkey and am absolutely delighted when I receive such rapturous response from my family and friends. Every year, I rise to the challenge of presenting a different taste and a different stuffing.

A friendly butcher once told me that a freshly-killed female turkey has more breast meat and will serve more people. I usually serve 20 people at a minimum. And even if there are fewer, I make the same amount of stuffing, because there never seems to be enough. You can freeze any extra stuffing and serve later as a side dish.

Ingredients

22	lbs freshly-killed female turkey
1	lemon for rubbing turkey
2	Tbsp liquid honey
2	Tbsp all-purpose flour

Method

The night before cooking, rinse the turkey with cold water and rub inside and outside with fresh lemon. Sprinkle with salt and pepper inside and out, and refrigerate.

The next day, before making the stuffing, rub honey inside the turkey and out. You could also use maple syrup or any other favourite spice for a different flavour, but be sure not to overdo it. You don't want the spice to be overpowering. Sprinkle flour over and rub it on turkey. Set aside.

Ingredients for Roasting Pan

1/4	cup butter
5-6	branches parsley
2	stalks celery
10	juniper berries
2	garlic cloves, halved
6	bay leaves
1	branch sage
1	branch rosemary
1-3/4	cups stock or water
1/2	tsp fresh ginger
10	black peppercorns

Add the ingredients to the roasting pan before baking. Stuff turkey with one of the following stuffings before baking.

Rita's Stuffing

Ingredients

3/4	lb wild rice
1/2	lb ground pork
1/2	lb ground goat or veal
1	tart apple, peeled and diced
1	garlic clove, minced
1	Belgian lettuce, chopped
1/4	cup raisins, washed and soaked in 1/2 cup brandy
1/4	cup walnuts, chopped
1/4	cup cornmeal
1	egg, slightly beaten
1	cup turkey stock or water
2	oz butter
3	Tbsp parsley, chopped
3	leaves fresh sage, minced
1	leek, white part only, chopped
2	tsp honey
	fresh ground pepper and salt to taste

Method

Rinse rice and cover with cold water. Bring to boil. Cover and set aside.

In a large frying pan, melt butter. Add pork, goat, garlic and leeks. Cook covered for 5 or 6 minutes, stirring occasionally.

Add and stir diced apples, lettuce, rice, stock or water and cook for about 5 minutes. Add raisins and walnuts, stirring for a few seconds.

Remove from heat and stir. Add cornmeal, parsley, sage, salt, pepper and brandy. Set aside to cool. After it has cooled, add the egg and stir. Spoon into the turkey cavity before trussing.

Wrap the wings and legs with pieces of foil paper to prevent overcooking. In a preheated 400° F oven, place covered turkey, breast-down and cook for an hour. Reduce heat to 350° F and turn the turkey breast-up. Baste again. Use a meat thermometer or cook to your liking, allowing 20 minutes per pound.

Remove turkey when done and set aside for 20 minutes in a tray. Strain the herbs, remove fat from the pan and use to make a gravy.

❖

Vodka Stuffing

Ingredients

		liver and heart of turkey, minced
1/4	tsp	cinnamon
1	Tbsp	salt
6	Tbsp	butter
1/4	lb	capiccollo, minced (Italian pork shoulder)
1		white onion, chopped
6		garlic cloves
1		cup spinach
3/4	lb	veal, minced
1		cup vodka
1		apple, diced
2	Tbsp	pinenuts, toasted
1/4	tsp	rosemary
6		sage leaves, chopped
3	Tbsp	parsley, chopped
1/2	tsp	tarragon
2		eggs, slightly beaten
2		cups breadcrumbs
		salt and pepper to taste

Method

Melt butter in a frying pan. Sauté liver, heart, onions, garlic, capiccollo and veal for a few minutes. Add spinach and breadcrumbs. Turn off heat. Stir vodka into mixture. Set aside to cool.

When cool, add pinenuts, rosemary, cinnamon, parsley, tarragon, salt and pepper. Finally add beaten egg and shape into a meat loaf. Spoon into cavity of turkey. Truss or stuff turkey with large lettuce leaf to hold stuffing in place.

Ingredients for Roasting Pan

2	whole apples
2	garlic cloves
4	bay leaves
1	peppercorn
6	cherry tomatoes
1	branch thyme
1	branch hyssop

Place in bottom of pan with a quarter of cup of oil or butter. Place turkey on top to roast.

In a preheated 400° F oven, place covered turkey, breast-down and cook for an hour. Reduce heat to 350° F and turn the turkey breast-up. Baste again. Use a meat thermometer or cook to your liking, allowing 20 minutes per pound.

Remove turkey when done and set aside for 20 minutes in a tray. Strain the herbs, remove fat from the pan and use to make a gravy. ❖

Italian Rice Stuffing

Ingredients

2		cups Italian rice (Vialone or Arborio)
1		fillet pork tenderloin (approx 1 lb)
4		cups borage
4	Tbsp	cornmeal
2		cooking apples, peeled and cut into chunks
1		parsnip, grated
3		white shallots
2		garlic cloves, minced
1	tsp	winter savory
10		chestnuts
2	oz	butter
2	oz	oil
4	oz	white wine
1		cup water
		salt and pepper to taste

Method

Pierce chestnuts. Cook for 10 minutes in a preheated 400° F oven. When cool, shell chestnuts.

Rinse the rice. Mix oil and butter in a wide pan. Add shallots, meat and rice, stirring over low heat for approximately 5 minutes. Add apples, chestnuts, borage, water and wine. Continue to sauté for another 5 minutes.

Remove from heat. Add cornmeal, savory, salt and pepper. Spoon into cavity. Truss or stuff large lettuce leaf in cavity to hold stuffing in place.

In a preheated 400° F oven, place covered turkey, breast-down and cook for an hour. Reduce heat to 350° F and turn the turkey breast-up. Baste again. Use a meat thermometer or cook to your liking, allowing 20 minutes per pound.

Remove turkey when done and set aside for 20 minutes in a tray. Strain the herbs, remove fat from the pan and use to make a gravy. ❖

Cranberry Sauce

(Salsa di mirtilli rossi)

Ingredients

2	lbs fresh cranberries, rinsed, washed and drained
1	cup cherry brandy
1	lemon rind, grated
1	cup sugar
1	cooking apple, grated

Method

Place all ingredients in a wide saucepan. Cook for 5-6 minutes over medium heat, stirring occasionally. Serve with turkey.

This can also be stored in sterilized jars. It also freezes very well and keeps up to a year. ❖

Marinated Mushrooms and Capers

(Funghi marinati con capperi)

Ingredients

5	lbs fresh mushrooms
4	cups white vinegar
1/2	cup coarse salt

Rinse out mushrooms and leave whole. Place in a dish and sprinkle salt over. Add white vinegar and mix well. Place a plate and a 5-lb load on top. Leave for 4-5 hours. Mix again, then replace load and leave overnight.

Drain mushrooms in a colander. Place dish and 5-lb load on top.

Dressing Ingredients

1/4	cup olive oil
1/2	cup capers, washed and rinsed
1/2	cup fresh peppermint leaves
2	Tbsp savory
5-6	sprigs rosemary
1	red sweet pepper, julienne
1	hot pepper, cut into rounds
2	Tbsp raspberry vinegar
2	garlic cloves, quartered

Mix all dressing ingredients. Pour over mushrooms. Mix well. This can be made ahead of time. Refrigerate and bring to room temperature before serving. ❖

Green Salad

(Insalata verde)

Salad Ingredients

2	heads Boston lettuce
2	heads Romaine lettuce
2	radishes, sliced
2	green onions, chopped
6	Tbsp fresh garlic chives, chopped
2	Tbsp tarragon

Dressing

4	oz olive oil
2	oz tarragon vinegar
2	tsp oregano

Method

Rinse, dry and cut lettuce. Place all salad ingredients in a salad bowl.

In a jar, shake all dressing ingredients well and pour over salad before serving. ❖

Easter Bread
(Pane di Pasqua)

Every Easter, for centuries, Easter bread has been baked. Every family has its own recipe, but the shape of the bread is not always the same.

The round "cuzupe" represents the family, and each child would place an egg on each twist to represent each member of the family. We use the imprint of an old key to devise different designs for the "cuzupe" and then brush it with icing sugar or egg before baking.

Makes 6 loaves

Ingredients

2	envelopes dry yeast
2	tsp sugar
1	cup lukewarm water

Dissolve sugar in water. Add yeast and cover. Let stand for 10 minutes.

3	cups warm milk
5	cups all-purpose flour, sifted

Add milk and flour to the yeast mixture, and whisk. Cover with a damp cloth. Let stand for 1 hour.

10	egg yolks	
6	eggs	
1/2	cup sugar	
1	Tbsp salt	
2	Tbsp vanilla	
1/4	cup cognac	
1	cup unsalted butter	
14	cups all-purpose flour, sifted	
1	egg yolk	for brushing
1	Tbsp cold water	before baking

Method

Blend remaining ingredients except the flour in a mixing bowl till yellow. Turn out flour on rolling board. Make a well in the centre. Add yeast mixture, then the egg mixture. With a rotating motion mix until all the flour is absorbed.

Knead for 8-10 minutes. Shape dough into a smooth ball. Place in a buttered bowl and cover with a linen cloth. Let stand for 1-1/2 hours in a warm place.

Take a piece of dough. Roll into a long strip 18" long. Braid into shape of horseshoe and place an egg on the top. Take 2 ends and twist them together.

Alternatively, divide into 6, then divide each into 3 strips. Braid 3 strips together to form one.

Let stand for another hour until each doubles in size. In a small bowl, mix egg yolks and 1 Tbsp of water. Then, brush the cooled bread.

Bake in preheated oven at 400° F for 10 minutes. Reduce heat to 350° F and bake for 35-40 minutes or until golden.

Lamb or Goat Tiella
(Tiella di capretto o agnello)

This is a very old recipe whose name is derived from the pan in which it is cooked. The "tiella" is a copper pan 4" deep and 10-15" in diameter. It has two handles and a tin cover about 2" bigger in diameter than the bottom of the pan (so they could place the coal and ashes on the cover).

When I was a child, the tiella was used only for special occasions. My grandmother would put the lamb and potatoes in the tiella, then shut the lid on which she would place ashes and coal. As a substitute for the traditional tiella, I use a large pan over a barbecue grill and a pizza tray for a lid, on which I place some coals.

Ingredients

4	lbs goat or lamb
2	ripe tomatos
1/2	cup white wine
4	garlic cloves, minced
1/2	cup parsley, minced
2	Tbsp breadcrumbs
6	potatoes, cut lengthwise
3	green onions, white part only, minced
1/4	cup olive oil
	salt and pepper to taste

Method

Place all ingredients in a pan. Mix with your hands until the meat is coated with the other ingredients. Put the lid in place. Place ashes and coal on top. Cook for 25-35 minutes until the aroma tells you that it's done. ❖

Cecilia's Chocolate Cheesecake

Ingredients

3-1/2	cups pecans
2	Tbsp flour
3	Tbsp Tia Maria
3	Tbsp brown sugar
1/4	cup butter
1	oz semi-sweet chocolate

Blend all ingredients at high speed for about 1 minute. With the back of a spoon, gently line a round 12" x 2-1/2" pan. Refrigerate for later use.

Filling

6	egg yolks
6	egg whites
1	cup sugar
1/2	cup whipping cream
2	pkg ricotta cheese (about 2 lbs)
3	Tbsp Tia Maria
1/4	tsp salt
2	oz semi-sweet chocolate, melted and cooled
2	Tbsp all-purpose flour
	rind of 1 tangerine, grated

Beat yolks and sugar for 5 minutes until creamy and lemon-coloured.

Add liqueur, ricotta, melted chocolate and flour. Continue beating at low speed until it is well blended. Blend in whipping cream and tangerine rind very quickly.

Beat whites and salt until peaks are formed. Gently fold them into the ricotta mixture. Bake in a preheated oven at 300° F for 1 hour or until cake bounces back to the touch.

Turn heat off. Leave in oven with door open for another hour.

Topping

1	cup whipping cream
2	Tbsp sweet chocolate, grated
2	Tbsp fine sugar

Place bowl and egg white beater in freezer for 5 minutes.

Remove from freezer. Place whipping cream in bowl. Start whipping at low speed. Add fine sugar gradually and continue whipping at higher speed until peaks form. Refrigerate.

Just before serving, spread whipping cream with spatula over cheesecake. Sprinkle chocolate over. ❖

Menu for Six

This menu was served when my husband's nephew and his wife came to visit us from Italy. The lemon ice cream can be bought from any Italian ice cream store, and was included because my husband's nephew is a representative for an Italian ice cream ingredient manufacturer.

DESPERATELY DELICIOUS RABBIT
POLENTA
BUTTERNUT SQUASH AND PEAS
FANTASIA SALAD
LEMON ICE CREAM
COFFEE

Desperately Delicious Rabbit

(Coniglio alla disperata)

I devised this recipe for my niece, Antonella, who so enjoyed my rabbit dishes that she wanted to learn to make it herself. The name for this dish is derived from the pains she took to make this dish. So much so, she was ready to tear her hair out! But the result of her efforts won much praise from her husband, Rocco.

Ingredients

1	4-lb rabbit
2	leeks, white part only
4	garlic cloves
1	tsp freshly ground ginger
1	hot pepper (optional)
1	apple, peeled and sliced
1	tsp dry savory
2	Tbsp parsley
1	oz sherry
2	tomatoes, peeled and seeds taken out, chopped
1/4	cup olive oil
1	Tbsp flour
1	oz white vinegar

Method

Cut rabbit in pieces and completely cover in cold water. Add 1 oz white vinegar. Let stand for 1 hour before draining.

Combine oil, leeks, garlic and rabbit in a wide frying pan. Cover for about 5 minutes over medium heat stirring occasionally. Uncover and stir until liquid evaporates.

Add ginger, apple, pepper and tomatoes, stirring constantly. Add sherry and sprinkle flour to thicken sauce, while turning with a wooden spoon. Place in serving dish and sprinkle with parsley. ❖

Polenta

This is a very healthy dish which is often associated with the North of Italy, but as children in Rogliano, we used to eat it quite often.

It was served with beans, chick peas, rabbit, quail and game. Leftovers were never wasted as they were grilled over the fire and served with sauce.

This dish can be made 2 or 3 days ahead and served hot or cold. Keep refrigerated but do not freeze.

Ingredients

8	cups water
3/4	lb cornmeal
1-1/2	tsp salt
2	bay leaves
2	Tbsp butter

Method

Combine water, bay leaves and salt in a pot. Bring to boil and cook covered for 2-3 minutes. Sprinkle cornmeal in the liquid, stirring constantly. Keep stirring for about 1/2 hour or until polenta does not stick to sides of the pot.

Add butter. Pour into serving dish.

Butternut Squash and Peas

(Zucca con piselli)

Ingredients

5	cups peas
5	cups butternut squash, cut into squares
2	fresh green onions, white part only, chopped
1/4	cup olive oil
2	garlic cloves, chopped
1/4	cup water
	salt and pepper to taste

Method

Place all ingredients in a pot. Bring to boil. Lower heat and simmer for 20 minutes, occasionally shaking the pan. ❖

Fantasia Salad

(Insalata fantasia)

Ingredients

1	head radicchio, washed and cut
2	heads Belgian lettuce, washed and cut
2	cooking apples, peeled and cut
1/2	head finocchio, cut finely lengthwise
1	white radish, sliced
1	small green onion, cut very fine
	salt and pepper to taste

Dressing

2	oz olive oil
1	oz raspberry vinegar
1	tsp oregano
1	garlic clove, squashed

Method

Place dressing ingredients together in a jar and shake well.

Place salad ingredients in a salad bowl. Just before serving, shake dressing well. Pour over salad. Mix well and serve. ❖

Special Treat Menu

Serves 6

This menu was prepared for a rare occasion. It combines the unusual flavour of moose with the lightness of the different kinds of vegetables and salad that I serve with it.

MOOSE STEAK

SWISS CHARD WITH FONTINA CHEESE

BEET WITH TARRAGON
(See Christmas Menu)

RADICCHIO SALAD

ANTIPASTO DIP

RHUBARB AND RASPBERRY FLAN

Moose Steak
(Bistecche di alce)

Ingredients

7	moose T-bone steaks (about 3 lbs)
1	cup dry red wine
3	leaves savory, chopped
1	sprig rosemary, chopped
3	sprigs parsley, chopped
5	leaves sage chopped
3	garlic cloves, minced
1	Tbsp olive oil
	salt and freshly ground black pepper to taste

Method

Rinse steak with 1/2 cup wine. Place steaks in dish and add remaining ingredients. Turn and marinate for 3 hours. Barbecue steaks to your liking. ❖

Swiss Chard with Fontina Cheese
(Coste alla fontina)

Ingredients

12	leaves swiss chard, washed and cut widthwise
1	Tbsp salt
3	Tbsp butter
3	garlic cloves, minced
2	medium onions, cut into rounds
2	Tbsp breadcrumbs
1	cup fontina cheese, grated
	salt and pepper to taste

Method

Fill pot with water. Bring swiss chard and 1 Tbsp salt to boil. Remove and drain in a colander.

In a frying pan, place butter, garlic and onions. Cook covered over low heat for 10 minutes until tender. Remove cover and add swiss chard. Stir.

Add breadcrumbs, cheese, salt and pepper to taste. Stir until cheese is melted. Remove and place in a serving dish. ❖

Radicchio Salad
(Insalata di radicchio)

Ingredients

4	heads radicchio, washed and broken with hands
2	small white onions, sliced into fine rounds
2	Tbsp mint leaves, chopped
4	leaves fennel, chopped

Dressing

1	garlic clove, minced
2	oz olive oil
1	oz raspberry vinegar
1	Tbsp oregano
	salt and pepper to taste

Method

Place all dressing ingredients in a jar and shake well.

Place salad ingredients in a salad bowl. Just before serving, shake dressing well. Pour over salad. Mix well and serve. ❖

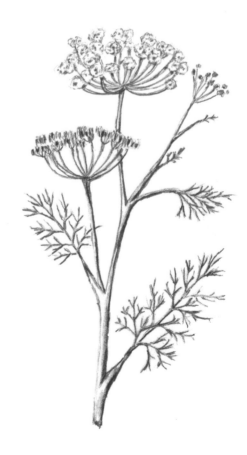

Antipasto Dip

This can be served with smoked salmon, vegetables or caviar.

Ingredients

1/2	lb feta cheese
1	cup milk
1	lb ricotta cheese
1	Tbsp olive oil
1/4	tsp cayenne
1/4	tsp white pepper
1	Tbsp hyssop flowers

Method

Soak feta cheese in milk for about half an hour. Drain milk from cheese.

Place all ingredients in a blender except for the hyssop flowers. Blend until creamy.

Place in a serving bowl. Add half the hyssop flowers and stir. Use the other half to decorate the dip. Cover and refrigerate until ready to serve. ❖

Rhubarb & Raspberry Flan

(Crostata di rabarbaro con lamponi)

Crust

3-1/4	cups soft wheat flour
3/4	cup butter
2	egg yolks
4	Tbsp sugar
1/2	cup cold water
1/2	tsp salt
	rind of 1 lemon

Method

Place flour on a rolling board. Make a well in the middle and add all other ingredients. Knead the dough to a nice smooth consistency. Refrigerate for at least an hour until ready for use.

Roll out dough on a floured board. Fold over and roll it out again. Repeat 2-3 times.

Stretch and cover flan dish. Use fork to pierce pastry. Spoon filling over.

Bake at 425° F for 10 minutes. Lower heat to 375° F for another 20 minutes.

Rhubarb Filling

4	cups rhubarb
1-1/2	cups sugar
	juice of 1 orange
1	oz Cointreau
1	cup raspberries
1	Tbsp corn starch

Wash rhubarb and cut into 1" lengths. Add all filling ingredients to a pan. Cook over medium heat for 1 minute, or until rhubarb is soft.

Raspberry Apple Filling

1	cup raspberry jam
4	large cooking apples
2	Tbsp sugar
1/4	cup Cointreau

Method

Core and slice apples into thin crescents.

In a frying pan, add jam, sugar and Cointreau. Stir over medium heat for 1 minute. Turn heat off. Cool.

Spread filling over flan crust. Arrange apple crescents in decorative patterns. Bake at 425° F for 10 minutes. Lower heat to 375° F and bake for another 15 minutes. ❖

Federico's 50th Birthday Menu

This was the menu I planned for my husband Federico's Surprise Birthday Party. In Italian custom, attaining the half-a-century mark is a red-letter occasion, and we invited many of his old friends.

ROAST PIGLET

EGGPLANT TIELLA

ASPARAGUS WITH MINT SAUCE
See Menu for Businessmen's Delight

RAPINI WITH LEMON

STUFFED BREAD

PIQUANT SALAD

STRAWBERRY BASKET

Roast Piglet

(Porchetta al forno)

Ingredients

1	30-lb piglet
8	cups water
1	cup vinegar
1/4	cup salt

The night before, remove the kidneys from the piglet. Rinse piglet in running cold water. Rub with salt, especially the ears, face and feet. Let stand for 10 minutes so the salt will penetrate. Rinse with the mixture of vinegar and water.

Herb and Spice Mixture

1	tsp coriander
1	tsp cayenne
1	tsp juniper
1	tsp dry fennel
1	tsp black pepper
1	tsp mustard seeds
1	oz olive oil

Grind all the above ingredients except the olive oil and place in a dish. Add olive oil. Mix. Rub piglet inside and out with herb and spice mixture. Refrigerate overnight.

Filling

1	lb wild rice
1/2	cup olive oil
1	white onion, chopped
3	garlic cloves, minced
1	pork tenderloin, chopped
2	tart apples, peeled, cored and chopped
1/2	cup golden raisins, washed
1	cup gin
1/2	cup pine nuts
3	Tbsp coarse cornmeal
1/4	tsp nutmeg
4	fresh caraway branches, minced
1	Tbsp fresh winter savory, chopped
	salt and pepper to taste

Method

Soak raisins in gin. Wash wild rice. Cover with cold water. Bring to boil and cook covered for 2-3 minutes. Stir. Turn heat off and set aside.

In a non-stick frying pan, add oil, onions, garlic and tenderloin. Fry over medium heat for 3 minutes. Add rice, and stir. Cook for 2 minutes. Add apples, raisins, gin and pine nuts, stirring all the time. When rice is cooked, add cornmeal, nutmeg, caraway, savory, salt and pepper. Cool.

When cool, stuff piglet with filling. Sew or skewer opening. Tie the back feet to the head.

Baking Ingredients

1	cup olive oil
1	cup water
5	sprigs parsley
2	sprigs rosemary
2	sprigs sage
4	sprigs thyme
15	juniper berries
6	bay leaves
6	slices fresh ginger
2	peppercorns
6	garlic cloves

Preheat oven to 400° F. Place all above ingredients in baking pan. Place piglet, side down on the pan. Cover ears of piglet with foil. Cover baking pan with foil.

Bake for 15 minutes. Reduce heat to 350° F and continue baking. Allow 20 minutes for each lb. Baste occasionally with drippings.

Halfway through cooking, turn piglet to the other side. Keep covered till the last 5 minutes. However, if you prefer skin to be crackling, remove foil 1/2 hour before cooking is done.

Remove filling onto a side dish. Place piglet in a dish as a centre piece. Guests may help themselves. ❖

Eggplant Tiella

(Tiella di melanzane alla Maria)

On September 7 every year, the town of Rogliano celebrates the feast of St. Mary by cooking all kinds of eggplant dishes. Of course, my mother used to cook the best eggplant in town, and we always had visitors who came just to savour it.

Ingredients

1-1/2	lbs medium eggplants, halved (about 4)
1	leek, white only, chopped
6	mushrooms, chopped
4	oz capicollo, chopped
10	green olives, pitted and chopped
1	Tbsp capers, washed and chopped
2	artichoke hearts, chopped
1	cup pecorino cheese
1	cup breadcrumbs
2	eggs
5	sprigs parsley, chopped
10	leaves sweet basil
1/4	tsp savory
2	garlic cloves, minced
1	cup scamorza cheese, grated
3	Tbsp butter
	salt and pepper to taste

Method

Cut eggplant in half and blanch in boiling water until fork-tender. Drain in colander and cool. Chop eggplant. In a bowl, mix with all other ingredients except butter.

Butter pan and pat mixture into shape. Add either topping.

Topping 1

2	medium tomatoes, sliced
1/2	cup scamorza cheese, grated
1/2	cup pecorino cheese, grated

Slice tomatoes and arrange on top of eggplant. Sprinkle scamoza and pecorino on top.

Topping 2

3	Tbsp olive oil
5	medium tomatoes, peeled and chopped
3	garlic cloves, minced
1/2	cup scamorza cheese, grated
1/2	cup pecorino cheese, grated
	salt and pepper to taste

Fry the garlic in olive oil for a few minutes. Add tomatoes and sauté for 3-4 minutes. Add salt and pepper to taste. Pour over eggplant. Sprinkle scamoza and pecorino on top.

Bake at 350° F for 1/2 hour, then broil for 2-3 minutes or until top is crusty. ❖

Rapini with Lemon

(Rapini con limone)

Ingredients

8	bunches rapini
2	Tbsp salt
40	cups water

Dressing

1/2	cup olive oil
6	garlic cloves, halved
1/2	cup parsley
	juice of 2 lemons
	rind of 1 lemon

Method

Trim bottom of rapini. Split in 2. Rinse and soak.

Bring a spaghetti pot of salt and water to boil. Add rapini and cook till tender. Drain in a colander.

Mix dressing ingredients. Pour over rapini when cool. Stir and serve.

This can be made a couple of days ahead and refrigerated. Bring to room temperature before serving. ❖

Stuffed Bread

(Pane imbottito)

Serves 6

In Italy, stuffed bread was served to those who worked on the estates of the landowners during the harvest season. This was often served with wine for breakfast.

In honour of my husband Rico's 50th birthday, I had the baker especially bake a double sized crusty bread for the occasion.

Ingredients

2	zucchini, de-seeded, sliced lengthwise
4	red peppers, cut lengthwise
2	yellow peppers, cut lengthwise
4	green peppers, cut lengthwise
2	hot peppers, cut lengthwise
2	large eggplants, cut lengthwise
4	potatoes, julienned
5	slices bacon
2	garlic cloves, minced
1/2	cup chives
1/2	cup chopped basil
1-1/2	cup olive oil
	salt and pepper to taste

Method

Place all vegetables in a large dish and sprinkle with salt. Place dish over. Let stand for an hour. Drain on absorbent paper towel.

In a frying pan, add oil and fry individual vegetables. Cook over high heat until vegetables are soft. Remove with a slotted spoon.

Drain oil and fry bacon, garlic and chives. Drain. Mix with vegetables. Add basil and mix well.

Slice about 1-1/2" off the top of the bread so it forms a lid. Remove insides and stuff bread with mixture. Cover with lid portion of bread.

Place in a serving dish and enjoy.

Piquant Salad

(Insalata piccante)

Ingredients

1	jar preserved artichokes
1	jar preserved mushrooms
1	jar hot peppers
1	jar preserved eggplant
1	jar green olives
1/2	cup parsley

Method

In a salad bowl, mix all drained ingredients and serve. ❖

Strawberry Basket

Ingredients

4	pints strawberries
3	Tbsp coarse sugar
10	lemon verbena leaves

Method

Wash strawberries and cut off tops. Drain in a colander. Shake until all water is drained off.

Decorate basket with embroidered linen. Fill with strawberries. Add verbena leaves and sprinkle with sugar.

❖

TABLES OF WEIGHTS & MEASURES

Solid Measures Conversion Chart

Liquid Measures Conversion Chart

Ounces	Pounds	Grams	Kilos	Fluid Oz	U.S.Measure	Imperial Measure	Millilitres
1		28			1 tsp	1 tsp	5
2		56		1/4	2 tsp	1 dessert-spoon	7
3-1/2		100					
4	1/4	112		1/2	1 tbs	1 tbs	15
5		140		1	2 tbs	2 tbs	28
6		168		2	1/4 cup	4 tbs	56
8	1/2	225		4	1/2 cup		110
9		250	1/4	5		1/4 pint or 1 gill	140
12	3/4	340					
16	1	450		6	3/4 cup		170
18		500	1/2	8	1 cup or 1/2 pint		225
20	1 1/4	560					
24	1 1/2	675		9			250
27		750	3/4	10	1 1/4 cups	1/2 pint	280
28	1 3/4	780		12	1 1/2 cups or 3/4 pints		340
32	2	900					
36	2 1/4	1000	1	15		3/4 pint	420
40	2 1/2	1100		16	2 cups or 1 pint		450
48	3	1350					
54		1500	1 1/2	18	2 1/4 cups		500
64	4	1800		20	2 1/2 cups	1 pint	560
72	4 1/2	2000	2	24	3 cups or 1 1/2 pints		675
80	5	2250	2 1/4				
90		2500	2 1/2	25		1 1/4 pints	700
100	6	2800	2 3/4	27	3 1/2 cups		750
				30	3 3/4 cups	1 1/4 pints	840
				32	4 cups or 2 pints or 1 quart		900
				35		1 3/4 pints	980
				36	4 1/2 cups		1000
				40	5 cups or 2 1/2 pints	2 pints or 1 quart	1120
				48	6 cups or 3 pints		1350
				50		2 1/2 pints	1400
				60	7 1/2 cups	3 pints	1680
				64	8 cups or 4 pints or 2 quarts		1800
				72	9 cups		2000
				80	10 cups or 5 pints	4 pints	2250
				96	12 cups or 3 quarts		2700
				100		5 pints	2800

NOTE: All conversions are approximate. They have been rounded off to the nearest convenient measure.

TABLES OF WEIGHTS & MEASURES

Oven Temperature Equivalents

FAHRENHEIT	GAS MARK	CELSIUS	HEAT OF OVEN
225	1/4	105	VERY COOL
250	1/2	120	VERY COOL
275	1	135	COOL
300	2	150	COOL
325	3	160	MODERATE
350	4	175	MODERATE
375	5	190	FAIRLY HOT
400	6	200	FAIRLY HOT
425	7	222	HOT
450	8	230	VERY HOT
475	9	245	VERY HOT

NOTE: Oven temperatures are given as degrees Fahrenheit throughout the text.

INDEX